Praise for
Maximize Your Prese...

"If you are hungry, and everyone in business today is hungry, *Maximize Your Presentation Skills* is for you. This book is motivational, inspirational, and jam-packed with information to take you to the top. Read it today."

—**Les Brown,** inspirational speaker and author of
Live Your Dreams and *Maximize Your Potential*

"Everybody needs to read this book! Lots of practical information presented in a succinct, witty, and readable way. Make the small changes that Kaye suggests—they will have big consequences."

—**Mark Victor Hansen,** cocreator of the #1
New York Times–bestselling series CHICKEN SOUP FOR THE SOUL,
and coauthor of *The One Minute Millionaire*

"Ellen is an absolute master at presentation skills. There is no one better to learn from."

—**Peter Lowe,** success strategist

"Outstanding! A must read for anyone in business today."

—**Naomi Rhode, CSP, CPAE,** former president,
National Speakers Association, and cofounder, SmartHealth, Inc.

"This book is like meeting Ellen in person. It's enthusiastic, professional, personable, and charismatic. You will love it."

—**Michael L. Wagner,** CEO, the Ohio Corn Growers Association

"A must read for any businessperson looking for better ways to communicate with people. Come to think of it, make that *every* business person!"

—**Robert L. Shook,** bestselling author of
Jackpot: Harrah's Winning Secrets for Customer Loyalty

"Kaye tells it all like it's never been told before: simple, smart, savvy. No matter what your profession, you can virtually see yourself succeed with her tried-and-true formula for success!"

—**Steven Wolfe,** chairman and CEO, Sneak Preview Entertainment

"*Maximize Your Presentation Skills* is like Ellen Kaye's personal coaching services: informative, authoritative, and friendly. You can't help but benefit from this book."

—**Jeff Davidson, M.B.A., CMC,** professional speaker and
author of *The Complete Guide to Public Speaking* and
The Complete Idiot's Guide to Managing Your Time

"The great thing about Ellen Kaye's book is that she covers behaviors and actions that are subtle, yet can completely change an impression and improve influence. You'll never be able to reach your potential as a presenter without drawing on her comprehensive insights for success."

—**Alan Weiss, Ph.D.,** author of *Million Dollar Consulting*

"Packed with fascinating and genuinely practical, useful advice that will give you the edge and ensure you get their attention! I had no idea business skills could be this sexy. Ellen's book is a great tool for giving your presentations some good old American pizzazz!"

—**Matt J. D. Anderson,** business management executive, Tetra Pak

"At the MAO Clinic, I meet and greet people all day who are ill and often angry and afraid. Ellen Kaye's suggestions really helped and redirected the way we do some things here."

—**Peggy Blake,** MAO Clinic ambassador

"Thank you, Ellen Kaye! She shares excellent, practical advice, and also a warm, human touch that makes it all feel so much more possible."

—**Karla Birkholz, M.D.,** board member,
American Academy of Family Physicians

Maximize Your Presentation Skills

How to Speak, Look, and Act on Your Way to the Top

Ellen A. Kaye

 THREE RIVERS PRESS • NEW YORK

To my father, Alvin "Cheerful Al" Kaye
with love and adoration

Published in the United States by Three Rivers Press, an imprint of the
Crown Publishing Group, a division of Random House, Inc., New York.
www.crownpublishing.com

THREE RIVERS PRESS and the Tugboat design are registered trade-
marks of Random House, Inc.

Originally published in the United States by Prima Publishing, a division
of Random House, Inc., Roseville, California, in 2002.

Interior design by Michael Tanamachi

Library of Congress Cataloging-in-Publication Data
Kaye, Ellen A.
     Maximize your presentation skills : how to speak, look, and act on
your way to the top / Ellen A. Kaye.
          p.   cm.
     Includes index.
     1. Business presentations. 2. Interpersonal communication.
3. Executives—Training of. I. Title.
     HF5718.22 .K39   2002
     658.4'52—dc21   2002066269

ISBN 0-7615-6352-0

10 9 8 7 6 5 4 3

Printed in the United States of America

First Edition

CONTENTS

ACKNOWLEDGMENTS

There are a host of people who have made this book possible and to whom I am deeply indebted. I am especially fortunate to have so many wonderful teachers, friends, and business associates, and I extend my heartfelt gratitude to each of them.

To Julia DeVillers for believing in me and then stepping down, forcing me to run the race myself.

To David L. Blackwell for your late-night telephone lectures urging me to continue. Thank you for your support, encouragement, and writing assistance.

To Carol Cushman, Marjorie Bair, Joseph Jastrab, Johnnie Belinda, and Marion Light for your love, guidance, nurturing, and faith in me.

To Robert G. Edelman and Dr. Christopher Traughber, the most wonderful brothers I never had. Thank you for always being there.

To Martin Culverhouse, GDMC, and Nicolas Farrier for your editing, enthusiasm, and dinners.

To Jeff Slutsky who loved me through thick and thin. To Jeff Herman, for your support, honesty, and continued friendship.

To David Richardson, my editor at Prima Publishing, for believing I could do it and taking a huge leap of faith. Thank you so much to Andrew Vallas, LauraMaery Gold, Kay Mikel, and the entire Prima team.

To Al Zuckerman, my literary agent, in advance, for making me a star.

To my father, "Cheerful Al" Kaye, a world famous gentleman. Thank you for your love and laughter, for your acceptance and generosity.

To my mother, Miriam Kaye, for her teachings.

To Dr. Ira and Babette Rubenstein for their continued love and support.

To Irving "Robby" Robinson for fueling my self-confidence.

To Sir Ira D. Kaye for his grand example as the ultimate entrepreneur.

To all of my clients, large and small, for honoring me with their trust and the privilege of collaborating with them. A special thanks to David M. Schneider, Albert "Al" Winn, and Addison "Buzz" Ellis.

INTRODUCTION

Becoming a successful leader is all about rules. I believe in teaching those rules—if for no other reason than that this knowledge will eventually enable you to break them. Learn the rules inside and out, and they will guide you in all situations.

While this book teaches the rules and how best to use them, it also shows you how and when to challenge, bend, and break them! Creativity consultant Roger Von Oech urges readers in his delightful and challenging book *A Whack on the Side of the Head* to think outside the box. In this book, I go one step further and urge you, once you know the rules, to *be* outside the box. This is creative leadership at its best.

Because you picked up this book and are reading this introduction, I know you have the desire to excel. Think about your goals. What are your dreams?

- A promotion
- A raise

- Increased self-confidence
- Respect
- Recognition
- Polish and poise

You name it. Read this book, do the work, and you will have the world at your feet.

Do you need this information? Ask yourself these questions:

- Is your career exactly where you want it to be?
- Are you confident in all situations?
- Do you always say what you mean, and mean what you say?
- Can you motivate others?
- If the Fortune 100 photographer caught you on camera today would you look polished, professional, and proud?
- Are you representing yourself and your company to the absolute best of your ability?
- When asked to give a speech at the last minute, or to do something for the chairman of the board, can you act confidently and graciously, and make the right lasting impression?

If you answered no to any of these questions, welcome to the human race! And if you're interested in winning the race, continue reading.

This book will save you time, money, and embarrassment and will shave years off your trip to the top. You are holding power, influence, and persuasion in your hands. To advance in leadership you need to *become* a leader. Your formal education will carry you only part of the way.

This book explores and explains the unwritten rules and how to master them. It's filled with fascinating and funny bloopers and outtakes from my coaching, seminars, and private classes. I reveal the big mistakes even CEOs and senior-level businesspeople make, and I show you how to avoid them.

My clients have always had access to the full benefit of the training, education, experience, and discipline I developed for my acting career. I've also shared with them insights, solutions, and methods that I have observed or created as a professional image consultant.

This book is packed with practical, easy-to-implement checklists, exercises, journaling topics, growth work, and answers to just about every situation you encounter in the business environment.

In today's extremely competitive, breakneck, media-driven world, you need to know specifically how to speak, look, and act as a leader. Everyone needs to learn these important skills and behaviors. They're the keys to powerful, accomplished leadership. Whether you are an entry-level beginner or a seasoned professional, you will find what you need in this book.

Entry-level future executive. You're just beginning to lead. You know you can do it. You believe in yourself. This book has the strategies, the ideas, the skills, the habits, and the insights you'll need to meet the challenges you will face.

Mid-level or junior executive. You've glimpsed the horizon, and you want to accelerate your career now. This book will help you discover and let go of what's holding you back, to speed up your success. Buy it, read it, keep it in your arsenal for situational reference. Make it your business bible.

Successful, savvy, seasoned leader. People are the investment you manage, and you can't personally train them all. But their excellence is a feather in your cap. Save time, save money. Your people need coaching. Make this handbook required reading for your entire group and see how they soar.

Don't depend on trial and error when it comes to your professional success. Honing your interpersonal skills, and improving how you speak, look, and act will exponentially increase your success, your leadership, and your peace of mind.

I've taught it. I've seen it happen. I believe in you!

Chapter 1

LEADERSHIP IMAGE

- Preplan Those First Impressions
- Body Works That Boost Your Image
- Create a Confidence Zone
- Clothes Do Make a Difference
- Control the Emotional Climate
- Use Timing to Your Advantage
- Potpourri

HAVE YOU EVER WONDERED WHY SOME PEOPLE seem to take charge so effortlessly? What is it about leaders that make us want to support their ideas? How do some people light up a room simply by walking in?

If you want to be a leader in your business, or if you just want to feel more self-confident in social situations, you have come to the right place. Some people seem to know "instinctively" what to do and how to act wherever they are. How do they do it? They learned how to do it—and you can too! All it takes is some honest self-evaluation, hard work, and belief in yourself. We start at the beginning, with first impressions. But there is much, much more to learn if you are reaching for success and power in yourself and in the workplace. You can't change the past, but you can certainly paint a brighter future for yourself. So decide what you need to work on and get on the fast track to success.

Preplan Those First Impressions

Here I come!
How do I make an entrance?

Your decision on how to enter depends on what you hope to accomplish. Think carefully about your goals. Do you want your entrance to be dramatic and high profile? Are you entering an important corporate meeting or a televised live Senate hearing? Are you entering a first meeting with a new client?

After considering your objectives and deciding what you want to achieve once inside, it's time to plan your entrance. When you want everyone to stop and notice your entrance, try this. Pretend it's Oscar night. Imagine you're a celebrity. Not hard, right? Time to make your Red Carpet Grand Entrance:

Beam. Turn up your charisma. Glow.

Exude confidence. Enter with all the "I'm hot" energy you have. Smile. Inhale deeply.

Count down. Three, two, one . . . Enter!

I want to sneak into a meeting and observe only. Any ideas?

Are you entering late during your new boss's important presentation to a small group of potential investors? Or do you have one of these challenges?

- You're wearing the same clothes as yesterday, except for the new pizza stain. *Embarrassing.*

- You are ill-prepared. *Ugh.*

- You forgot the documents you need. *Shame on you.*

- You're very late. *Double shame.*

- You haven't finished reading this book. *Unforgivable!*

If your goal is to slide into a meeting unseen and unobserved, here's the blueprint for Ellen's Ninja Entrance:

Think stealth. Before you enter, arrange your accoutrements. Remove coats, scarves, gloves, and so forth. Pull out your pen and paper from your briefcase, put on your glasses, have your reference materials handy.

Think invisible. Get very still; calm your thoughts and body. Control your breathing. Bring your aura, your energy, in very tight. Only when you have mastered yourself should you enter the room.

Be invisible. Enter from the rear of the room. Be seated in the first, most convenient, empty seat. Furtively glance around to see if you can acquire a copy of the agenda if you don't already have one. Then get busy with listening, reading the agenda, and writing notes, so you melt in unnoticeably.

Do not look around. Others may be watching you. Don't rustle your things. Be quiet, sit still, and listen intently. Don't even whisper to the person next to you. Try to catch up with whatever was happening prior to your arrival. At the first break, ask someone to help you get up to speed.

How do I make a good first impression?

First impressions count. In the first instant people see you, they form an initial opinion. Once an impression is formed, it is very hard to change. You want that first opinion to be favorable. To accomplish this, project a positive, professional image.

Right now, before you have to prepare for another meeting or speech, take a hard, objective look at who you are. Consider *everything:* your entrance, your image (which includes posture, voice, breathing, breath, scent, clothing, colors you wear, confidence, and charisma), your introduction, your handshake, your focus, your eye contact, your conversation, your character, your concentration, your preparation, your intention, your intelligence, your timing, your consideration, your content, your humor.

I'm meeting a client for the first time. How can I start a conversation?

Making contact with another person for the first time is an opportunity for a mutually beneficial relationship. It is a situation full of potential and profitability. This new client may be your best client for many years to come. Start off on the right foot by using this step-by-step guide for initiating a conversation:

1. Begin your meeting by introducing yourself in a clear, audible voice.

2. Offer a solid (not bone-crunching or dead-fish) handshake, a kiss, or a bow, as appropriate.

3. Thank your client for seeing you, and make some sort of acknowledgment or compliment showing knowledge of or respect for the client's status and position. "Thank you for meeting with me. It is such an honor to meet you." Or "I have heard about your excellent work."

4. Confirm the agenda. "Ms. Thomas, we planned to discuss the schedule of the training program I am going to conduct for your firm. Does that agenda still work for you?"

5. Be responsive to the answer and the degree of urgency. New, more pressing issues may have arisen.

6. Begin to create rapport by asking light, informational, unemotional questions. Stick with those that are easy to answer, friendly but not intrusive. "How was your flight?" "Have you been to [your city] before?" "What was the weather like in [their city] before you left?" "How long are you planning to stay?" These are always appropriate questions, even if they're not nearly as much fun as "Do you wear boxers or jockeys?"

7. If you feel it is appropriate, in time, you may establish a more personal rapport. However, be aware of any hesitancy on your client's part to become too personal. If your client indicates any

Ellen's Hot Tips

Keep Your Focus on Your Client

What is wrong with this conversation with your client? List all the problems.

I came here today to discuss my newest product, but I've been working in the basic systems division for two years. Six months ago, my company moved me to this product, and it's been exciting for me to learn about it and see it take off. I enjoy becoming well versed in a topic, and I like answering the questions that come up. Let me start with my overview.

Why doesn't this work? Examine where the focus and attention is here. Count the number of times you have said "I, me, my, mine." The focus is all wrong. It must be on the client, not on you.

Reframe your thinking. It is not all about what *you* have done, where *you* have been, what *your* goals are, what *you* enjoy, or what *you* want to do. Replace the Golden Rule with the Platinum Rule, created by Dr. Tony Alexandra. The Platinum Rule states: "Do unto others as they'd like done unto them." In other words, treat others as *they* would like to be treated.

discomfort or awkwardness, any reluctance at all, immediately redirect the conversation as gracefully as possible—to business. Avoid sex, politics, and religion, unless invited!

8. When it is your turn to speak, be concise and specific.

9. Make it all about your client.

My hands are full and I'm being introduced to someone new. What should I do?

Don't panic. Immediately smile and give a warm verbal greeting. (Or go Euro: Kiss kiss. Go Alaskan: Rub noses.) Better yet, grimace gently and apologize quickly for having your hands full. Shaking hands while holding things will show others you don't fully value the introduction. Instead, excuse yourself quickly and put things down so you are able to shake hands properly. Simply say, "Please excuse me for just a second while I put these down. I'm so happy to have the opportunity to meet you." If you must set your things on a coworker's desk, or within another person's realm, ask her permission and thank her. Everyone will notice your courtesy.

In the United States, as in many countries abroad, you must always have your right hand available to extend for a gracious handshake. A good handshake may be ruined by

Ellen's Hot Tips

Practice Keeping Your Right Hand Free

Your right hand must always be available to give a welcoming handshake. This can be tricky. Practice at home holding a stemmed wine glass or an old-fashioned glass, a napkin and a cocktail plate, or a full-size buffet dinner plate—in your left hand. Balance and maneuverability are important; you will look and feel much more confident and comfortable when you find yourself in social situations that include food or beverage service if you have mastered this skill at home.

holding food or drink, or having soiled hands, sticky fingers, or a cold hand from holding a chilled glass.

Body Works That Boost Your Image

How do I shake hands? (And why does it matter?)

First, why it matters. You are offering your hospitality. You're making up. You're confirming your agreement. This

9

is often the first expression of your personality and confidence. Historically, people shook hands to show that neither had weapons up their sleeves. Traditionally, a gentleman would never shake a lady's hand until she extended it first. If she did not, hand shaking would not happen. If a modern woman encounters a traditional gentleman, she should initiate the handshake. Contemporary women expect to shake hands.

Now, here is the basic technique. Extend your right hand, thumb up, your four fingers together. Firmly, without crushing any bones, grasp the other person's extended right hand. Give it one quick, tiny pump, and release. Keep these additional points in mind:

1. **Hands should be at room temperature, clean, and dry.** If enjoying a beverage, hold it in your left hand so your right hand is free to shake hands. If eating finger food, eat quickly and wipe your hands immediately on a cocktail napkin to keep them free of crumbs and sticky stuff. Wash your hands often, and always after using the restroom.

2. **Nervousness often manifests in sweaty or clammy hands.** Anyone who suffers from this condition is absolutely traumatized by the ritual of the handshake. If you are on the receiving end of a sweaty or clammy handshake, do not in any

way indicate you even noticed. Have some compassion: Smile politely and simply ignore it.

3. **Many men grab a woman's hand too tightly.**
Don't be so macho; lighten up. It will certainly be a plus for you in her eyes. It is rude and disrespectful to hurt someone, especially when doing it slyly within the context of a meet-and-greet handshake. If someone shakes your hand too hard and it hurts, quietly let him know. You're not doing the crusher a favor by ignoring it.

Traditionally, one should *never* refuse a handshake. But it's becoming more and more common for people to meet and greet without shaking hands. Why, you might ask? The more we know about how easily germs are transmitted, the more people are shying away from handshakes. Howard Hughes pioneered this practice. Donald Trump is now in the lead of this social trend, along with many doctors. Although the germ thing is real, it is pretty much resolved by the European tradition of a kiss on each check. Although I love this tradition, I can't quite see Americans kissing in the boardroom just yet.

I suggest that when sneezing, coughing, or yawning you cover your mouth by using the inside crook of your elbow rather than your hands. If you have a cold, the flu, or are coming down with anything, *never* sneeze or cough into your hand and then offer it. Give the rest of us a break. Say, "I have a cold today, so I am going to spare you." This is the only courteous way to handle the germ issue. And always carry a package of tissues.

Finally, when it comes to hands, keep your nails clean and manicured. Don't bite your nails, don't pick your cuticles, don't touch your hands to your face, head, ears, or nose—especially your nose. Don't rest your chin or head on your hand. Don't play with your hair. Double don't scratch: anything, anywhere, anyplace.

Avoiding Sweaty or Clammy Hands

Ellen's Hot Tips

While waiting to shake hands, do not keep them in your pockets; they may get sweaty or clammy. One of my clients swears by the following method of preventing sweaty palms: Swing your arms around behind you. If right handed, take your forefinger and thumb of your left hand and clasp them around the wrist of your right hand. Hold with pressure.

Chiropractors tell me sweaty palms can be caused by spinal misalignment. Consider seeing a chiropractor if you suffer from sweaty palms.

How should I sit (and stand) confidently?

Both sitting and standing confidently require excellent posture. Sounds old-fashioned, yes? It is, and it works. These days most of us spend too much time stressed out, hunched over our computers, shoulders tense and pulled up around our ears, heads pronated forward like monkeys, stomachs sticking out. Need I go on?

If you are still not convinced posture matters, or makes a difference in how others perceive you, prove the power of good posture. Walk into a room full of strangers with your shoulders hunched over, chest sunken in, belly extended. Carefully observe others' reactions to you. Then try the reverse: shoulders back, chin up, chest out.

The response you get is guaranteed to be completely different. People feel your energy, see your body position, and respond positively at a primal level. Get a handle on your posture and use other people's positive responses to your advantage.

Now, check your own posture. Get naked in front of a full-length mirror—this may be scary, but do it anyway. Stand about 2 feet away, turn sideways, and stand as you always do. Check yourself out. Although this may be difficult, remember this: Everyone else sees your posture; it's high time you did, too. Adjust your posture. This is your opportunity to get it right.

In a perfect world, your standing posture should look as follows. The top of your head should be parallel with the floor. Keep your chin up, both physically and psychologically. When looking straight ahead, the middle of your ear should be in alignment with the middle of your shoulder, hip, knee, and ankle. Keep your feet flat on the floor, parallel to each other, toes forward. Think: plumb line.

When sitting down, sit still, breathe deeply, and look in control (even if you're feeling totally flipped out). Your back should be straight against the back of the chair. Rest your arms gently on the armrests with feet flat on the floor, about 10 to 12 inches apart, toes forward. No fidgeting, nervous kicking, bouncing your knees, shaking your legs, or playing with your glasses, your pen, your soda, your keys, or pocket change. For women in skirts, keep those knees together at all times. Over the course of really long meetings, it's easy to forget. However, as more and more meetings are held behind glass walls, you may have a larger audience than you think.

Ellen's
Hot Tips

Perfect Posture for Standing

Balance a large, heavy, closed book on your head and try to keep it there while walking across the room, going up and down stairs, and turning. If the book stays on your head, your head is in the correct position. Congratulations!

Consider wearing trousers or a somewhat longer skirt than usual if you are expecting to sit in front of spectators.

What do I do with my hands?

If you want to have any career at all, especially if you want to fast track, you must know what your hands and body are doing at all times. This sounds easy, but when we get

How to Avoid the Hand Jive Jitters

Ellen's Hot Tips

Keep your hands out of your pockets. It generally draws attention in all the wrong ways. Likewise, avoid scratching or fidgeting with buttons, zippers, glasses, pens, or other objects.

Videotape yourself. If your arms and hands are relaxed at your sides, now and only now are you ready to start to consider using your hands to reinforce your speaking points.

To observe good use of hands, watch old black-and-white movies. Classic actors were trained properly, and they knew how to use their bodies to best advantage. Even in the most dramatic moments, they held their bodies still with their hands relaxed at their sides.

nervous, our hands suddenly become clumsy and cumbersome. They may take on a life of their own. Every movement, every gesture, even nongestures, may seem awkward. Unless you have been professionally coached and videotaped and know precisely what to do with your hands and arms, keep them relaxed, at your sides, and totally still.

How do I make eye contact without staring too much?

Staring and eye contact are completely different. It's staring only when you don't show any emotion. So look everyone straight in the eyes, and always do it with a smile. Let yourself be known through your eyes; they are the windows to your soul. Show emotion. Assuming you are conscious, think about what the speaker is saying. Look, listen, respond, and blink normally. Staring will never be a problem if you allow yourself to become engaged with the speaker's ideas.

Create a Confidence Zone

I'm always uncertain about how to prepare for big events. How can I feel more confident?

Utilize the Pre-Event Planning Organizer and you won't feel left out or worry again. I have designed this super

Pre-Event Planning Organizer

Ellen's Checklist

1. **Call the event organizer.** To make the most of every professional and social event, as soon as you receive the invitation, call the host.

2. **Thank the organizer for including you on the guest list.** Even if the organizer was required to invite you, it is thoughtful of you to express your appreciation.

3. **Inquire about the guest list.** Who else is invited? How many do they expect will show up? Who should you try/hope to meet?

4. **Be sure you understand the dress code.** The invitation says: "cocktail" or "formal" or "casual." If you don't know exactly what this means, don't be afraid to ask. "By the way, what exactly does that mean here in (New York City, Wichita, Kansas, Beijing, Phoenix in July)?"

5. **Inquire about the agenda of the event.** Who is doing what, when?

6. **Collect timing tips.** What is the time schedule? At what time are guests invited? Even more important, when are most guests realistically

(continues)

(continued)

expected to arrive? And leave? How much time
is scheduled for each event on the agenda? How
long will cocktails last? Who will speak first?
For how long? Will a strict schedule be adhered
to, or is everyone allowed to go overtime if they
so choose?

7. **Check to see if there is a "no-host" bar.** If so,
you must remember to bring ready cash to pay
for drinks. Have small bills so you don't have a
problem getting change. Remember, each time
you get a drink, or a group of drinks, it is an expected courtesy to leave a tip for the bartender.
(Thinking you might be able to skip the tip?
Wrong.)

8. **Ask about the food format.** Is it a buffet or a sit-
down dinner? Is there assigned seating, or is it
first come, first served? Are there both hot and
cold hors d'oeuvres? Will food be served throughout the event, or is serving stopped at a certain
time? If so, ask what time that is. If only cold
hors d'oeuvres are being served, you may want
to have a small snack before you arrive. If you
haven't eaten all day, perhaps a large glass of milk
is in order, depending on your evening plans.

checklist to help you ask the right questions and then keep track of what you need to know.

If you make it a habit to use this list faithfully, you'll always know what's what, who's who, where, and when. In fact, some of my clients have used this method so successfully they tell me others think of them as the source of information.

I'm uncomfortable meeting new people. How can I develop more self-confidence?

Self-confidence is developed incrementally. Make the time and commitment to develop your self-confidence. Start now and you will benefit from it each and every day of your life, both personally and professionally. Don't kid yourself; it's not easy, but it is possible. And well worth it. Actively developing a healthy self-image is

> *A journey of a thousand miles begins with a single step.*
>
> —Lao-tzu, famous Chinese communication and image coach

a very good thing. Use my checklist on How to Develop Greater Self-Confidence to start your program of personal development.

Ellen's Checklist

How to Develop Greater Self-Confidence

1. **Take some time for your own personal self-development.** Do a complete inventory on your self. Look at your opportunities and your strengths. Evaluate yourself and keep the results. Make a 1-year plan and work on it daily, weekly, monthly. Do this over the years and look at your growth.

2. **Courage counts. Jump in!** The best way to develop self-confidence is to take the opportunity to introduce yourself or express your ideas. If your performance is not your best, or your idea gets shot down, you will survive. Confident people take a bad response in stride. A rebuff doesn't diminish you. Adapt and learn from it.

3. **Take an acting class, acting for nonactors, or improvisation.** Learning how to act will help free up your creativity, imagination, and self-appreciation. It will also help you get in touch with your spontaneity and your aliveness.

4. **Create positive rituals in your life, for you alone and with family and friends.** Ritual develops and feeds our human need for belong-

ing, tradition, meaning, and control. Make rituals that are comforting, supportive, and easy to maintain. For example, take 20 minutes each morning to stretch, or write in your journal, or plan your day—or all three.

5. **Integrate gratitude and celebration into your daily life.** Actually write down what you are grateful for at the beginning or end of every day. Recognize and appreciate the many good things you are blessed with each day. Be grateful for all of your own efforts. Celebrate every growth step.

6. **Think positively.** Clear your mind of all worry—so easy to say, so hard to do. Focus on what you really want. Whatever you focus your thoughts and energy on is what you attract.

7. **Find a topic interesting to you and relevant to others. Learn it well.** Develop a few lead-in statements to use as introductions to this topic for suitable moments. Start a conversation about your topic when the opportunity arises. Each small success will lead to another.

8. **Contact a trusted friend before and after doing a challenging task.** Get that person's

(continues)

(continued)

support and advice prior to the task, and afterward seek out congratulations, praise, a kick in the backside, or condolences. This technique of getting encouragement before and feedback after is called "book-ending." As you engage in challenging book-ending tasks, you will become more confident and independent.

9. **Start investing in yourself immediately.** Don't be afraid to invest time and money in workshops and personal growth seminars. At work, request a budget for professional workshops, seminars, and courses. Most of corporate America recognizes the value of professional training and coaching. Consider this an investment in your future.

10. **Read.** Read the top fifty classic books. Read self-help books. Read whatever fascinates you and whatever will educate you.

11. **Focus on the positive.** Always keep a good thought in your mind. Remember that worry is praying for what you don't want. The more you know about who you are, your values, and your priorities, the easier it will be to go after what you really want in your life and in your career.

I am a little bit overweight but can't seem to stay on my diet. Are there any ways to fool the eye?

By improving your posture, you can instantly appear to have lost 10 pounds, look taller, smarter, richer, and more powerful. Those who slouch may appear weak, sloppy, and stupid.

When buying and wearing clothes, keep in mind that darker colors, especially black, as well as monochromatic outfits, can be very slimming. Also, be sure to wear only what really fits. Nothing pulling or puckering at the seems, too tight, or too snug. Don't squeeze into anything. Make sure there is ample room across your back to reach for something without ripping a seem. Men watch that belly. No rolls over the top of your trousers or buttons so tight they are ready to pop. Shirt cuffs should graze the top of the indentation between your thumb and forefinger. Trousers should be long enough to break at your instep.

People say that wisdom comes with age, but I can't wait! How can I discover more about who I am right now and use that knowledge to increase my confidence?

To discover and define who you are and what you want, it helps to start a journal. I recommend writing down everything: the good, the bad, and the ugly. Sometimes it is difficult to assess yourself. If so, take a step back and pretend you are evaluating someone else. Write down all the characteristics you feel are unique to you. Consider yourself as a precious work of art. What makes you beautiful? Talented? Creative? Unique? Interesting? Fun? Fascinating? Different? So highly sought after? Worth so much?

Review your upbringing and education. Write about some of your best, funniest, and fondest memories. List the pivotal events and people in your life and education. Briefly describe who influenced you, how, and why their influence had a lasting impact.

Appraise your personal style. What charity do you work with? Collect for? Donate to? How do you give back to society? Are you a gracious host? Do you initiate events and get-togethers? Do you join along when invited? Take others out? What are your hobbies and special interests? Do you make them known? Share them with your colleagues? Are photos of some of your exciting experiences in a visible spot in your office? Or do you keep to yourself?

Look at your behavior and patterns in relationship to others. Are you a joiner? An isolationist? A libertarian? Do you connect with people?

> *Whatever you do, love yourself through it all. Love yourself every minute.*
>
> —*Marion Light, healer and massage therapist, Scottsdale, Arizona*

How? Around what? Do you make friends and keep them? Or do you prefer to go solo? Do you get out there?

Evaluate your professional behavior. Do you volunteer to help others? Do you stay late? Do you go the extra mile? Decide what works and what doesn't work for you and your life now. Make decisions for your highest good. If something does not work, get rid of it. Whatever it is—clothes, shoes, old habits, individual beliefs, whole belief systems, old tapes, parental rules and admonitions, self-limiting beliefs, furniture, old stuff—toss it. Keep what works and discard the rest. You're in the big leagues now—or close—it's time to clean up your act.

Remember, nature abhors a vacuum. So as you begin to clear out, you create space for something better to come in.

Ellen's Hot Tips

Exercise for Self-Discovery

Self-exploration results in greater self-knowledge, which results in greater self-confidence, which means more success. Here are a few tips for starting your journey:

1. Create a quiet physical and mental space in which you examine your rules, values, beliefs, boundaries, and ideals.

(continues)

(continued)

2. Are you getting and giving the best you possibly can? If not, start to reevaluate those ideas, constraints from the past, negative opinions, and drains on your energy and spirit.

3. Do some journaling. Write your stream of consciousness. Try writing your favorite life stories or experiences with the hand you don't usually write with. This is a cool trick to fool your subconscious; see what comes up for you.

4. Take my workshop, do some guided exploration, join a group with common interests, get private coaching or counseling. Read great books. Expand your horizons and open up new options.

The goal is to feel comfortable within your own skin, your body, your mind, and your spirit. Discover and develop who you are. Explore and uncover the real you. And then build on that big time.

Sure, we all think old habits are hard to break, but consciousness is instant. If you have the will, the commitment, and the desire, you can and will change. Once you have started the process, congratulate yourself and celebrate! You deserve it.

I want to be really confident.
What can I do for a confidence boost?

Use the power of music. Music immediately puts you in a very specific mood. Hearing just the first few bars of a piece of music can completely alter your emotional state.

Ellen's Hot Tips

Discover Your Mood-Motivating Music Triggers

To discover and keep track of your specific mood motivators, explore and indulge your musical tastes. Fill in your own Mood Music Trigger Chart to help you pinpoint which specific song, lyrics, genre, or singer's music triggers a definable mood and mind-set. If several pieces seem to elicit the same kind of feeling, always choose the strongest and most dramatic to assure that you create the feeling you want. Turn up your tunes, close your eyes, and experiment with finding the right music to inspire you to ask for that long-deserved raise, speak up at the upcoming staff meeting, or overcome the fear of dealing with your new supervisor. Here are some suggestions to get you started.

(continues)

(continued)

Mood Music Trigger Chart

EMOTION	SONG/MUSIC
Confident	*We Are the Champions* (Queen) *Gonna Fly Now—Theme from Rocky* (Bill Conti)
Powerful	*Hail to the Chief* (Albert Gamse) *These Boots Are Made for Walkin'* (Nancy Sinatra)
Inspired	*I Am Woman* (Helen Reddy)
Relaxed	*Don't Worry, Be Happy* (Bobby McFerrin)
Happy and carefree	*Margaritaville* (Jimmy Buffett)
Romantic	*Let's Face the Music and Dance* (Frank Sinatra)

Once you have determined your personal mood-motivating music triggers, play them immediately prior to an event to get you in the most appropriate frame of mind to deal most effectively with the issues at hand.

Rap music may pump you up. Sinatra may stimulate a sensual sway in your walk. A great symphony may inspire creativity. A march may make you feel powerful or patriotic. R&B may mellow you out. Hearing your prom song may trigger romantic reminiscing.

As you respond to music, you quickly change and direct your emotional state to your advantage. At work, this is a benefit to you as you prepare for meetings, presentations, and team projects. By selecting the appropriate trigger music, you will be able to put yourself into the right mood to deal with your daily challenges more effectively.

How can I be powerful today? This is my chance to shine.

Adopt the Boy Scout motto: Be prepared. Focus your preparation on these three areas: content, mental and spiritual issues, and logistics.

Content preparation. The biggest confidence boost is simply knowing your material.

- Review your material and facts until you've got them down cold.

- Do a Q&A with yourself.

- Practice with someone else asking you the questions that might be addressed.

Mental and spiritual preparation. Tap into your internal resources to improve your performance.

- Work out each step carefully and in detail. Mentally choreograph every move.

- Visualize the results you want. See yourself succeeding. Hear the praise. See the audience coming to you with smiles on their faces, wanting to congratulate you for your excellent work. Hear your boss's praise and thanks for a job well done.

Logistics preparation. The following logistical steps will help you radiate success:

Getting Ready to Do Your Best

Ellen's Hot Tips

To help you be at your best, I recommend the following for the night before and the morning of:

Pray. To express gratitude for the opportunity and ask for help.

Meditate. To quiet your mind and refresh your body.

Sing. To free your voice and spirit.

Exercise or stretch. To calm and loosen your body.

- Sleep. The night before and the morning of: review, rest, and relax.

- Eat properly.

- Be on time or early. Actually, early *is* on time.

- Rally support. Have allies present who support your goals.

I want to be the hero, the one to solve the big problems. How can I establish this reputation now?

To be a hero you have to ask the appropriate questions at the right time, and listen well to the answers. Glenna Salisbury, an internationally respected motivational speaker, showed this kind of leadership when she was scheduled to speak at Three Mile Island, the nuclear power plant in New York. Prior to her talk, a nuclear disaster occurred at the plant. Ms. Salisbury had the insight and courage to jettison her prepared speech. She researched the attitudes and fears generated by the accident and spoke directly to those issues. She dealt with the realities of the moment and did a great deal of good. This is real leadership.

If you want to solve the big problems, start now. Look at your work environment and evaluate the biggest, worst, most stressful unresolved issues in the company. What unspoken challenges need to be handled? Why are these problems still unresolved? What attempts have been made to solve them? Why did they fail? What is the ideal resolution?

Read between the lines. Strategically plan solutions to challenges on the table. Even better, figure out how to prevent future problems from arising. Read everything you can about successful leaders in war, in politics, in your field, in sports, in history, internationally. Learn about successful companies, and about failures. Study charismatic personalities, teamwork, the psychology of leadership, managing and motivating. Everything.

Watch everyone. Learn what works, what doesn't, and why. Then step up to the plate and act.

Clothes Do Make a Difference

"Dressing up" in a suit and tie seems like a total waste of time, money, and energy. Why bother?

It's true that Ted Turner and Bill Gates generally show up in khakis and a golf shirt. And somehow, they've managed to be successful in spite of it. But for everyone else, "clothes make the man." Cliché or not, they also make the woman. Although clothing should not have any effect on intelligence, productivity, or probability of success, your cloth-

Learn from Watching the Pros

Ellen's Hot Tips

Start watching the pros on television and in movies. What do they wear? Watch an interview by the hosts on *60 Minutes* or by Barbara Walters, Oprah, or Diane Sawyer. Whether you like them or not, they are always dressed to the nines while on television performing their jobs. Do their clothes correspond to their profession? You'll find the more professional the position, the more they respect the implicit "uniform" of their chosen profession.

ing is considered an extension of you, an external representation of who you are inside. So, "look sharp, feel sharp, be sharp."

Like it or not, clothing does unconsciously affect how you see and judge others. More important, if affects how others judge you. Experts get more respect, money, and attention by dressing the part. Professionals subtly show respect for their position and their audience by "dressing up." Make it easier for yourself and others: Look the part of the expert. After all, don't you want more respect, more money, and more attention?

I've been told I need to upscale my appearance. What does that mean?

It's time to take a look at the bigger picture: your posture and your wardrobe.

Before we review your wardrobe, it is important to observe the way you position yourself when you sit or stand (see page 13). Posture is a very important part of a powerful, professional image. People who hold themselves beautifully exude confidence and look powerful and desirable. We all subconsciously influence how others see and treat us. Having spent care and time on yourself, you are almost guaranteed to get better service.

Now on to your wardrobe. Your wardrobe includes more than simply your clothing. In addition to choosing clothing that complements your overall appearance, consider your accessories. Jewelry should be simple, tailored, and classic. No brightly colored dangling earrings, clinking bracelets, or large necklaces. A scarf or tie should be subtle, never overpowering or distracting. No theme ties. Makeup should be simple and natural. If you are going to wear a scent, be sure it is not overwhelming. Attire should be spotless, well pressed, and conservative. Shoes should always be well heeled, polished, and appropriate. Dress a level or two above your audience. If your audience members are wearing suits, you want to wear a great suit. If they want you in business casual, you want to be at the highest end of business casual you can. Generally this means a quality sport coat, pants, and no tie. Don't rely on advice from your parents or loved ones. Consult a professional.

Another very telltale item is your briefcase. Some of my clients pride themselves on carrying the same briefcase throughout their career. If your briefcase still looks

Tailor Your Clothing to Your Career

Ellen's Hot Tips

What you wear depends on the who, what, where, when, and why of your schedule, your life, your goals, and your career. Your professional wardrobe needs to be appropriate to your professional environment, budget, and lifestyle; supportive of your intentions; in harmony with your personality; and flattering to your coloring and body type (height, weight, and build).

When looking at clothing, especially business wear, you generally get what you pay for. An expensive suit, properly made with quality material, will give you many more years of looking great than an inexpensive suit. Look for quality, cut, and value, not just price. When in doubt, err on the side of conservatism.

terrific and represents you and your company well, great. If not, get rid of it now. Buy a new one that looks just the way it should for the professional leadership image you want to create.

My budget is limited. How important is footwear? Can I save some money here to spend on other parts of my wardrobe?

No! Footwear is not the place to scrimp or cut corners. There's only one thing you need to wear to work: a good pair of shoes. People love shoes. People look at shoes. People judge you by your shoes. The phrase "well heeled" describes someone who is well dressed, polished, and professional.

The person who attends to and has pride in a professional image and wardrobe is perceived as someone who will bring the same integrity and attention to detail to business responsibilities. That's a persuasive reason to pay attention to your shoes, yes? You can wear an expensive suit and a $30,000 watch, but if your shoes curl at the toe or look beat up, you've lost the entire image game.

There are several things you should know about purchasing shoes. First, buy quality shoes. Wear shoes of the same quality as your other clothing items, or better, since they are such a mark of distinction. If you have a limited budget (and who doesn't these days?), putting money into quality shoes is a good place to invest. (As a trade off, buy

Ellen's Hot Tips

Create Your Personal "Look Book"

A top executive complained to me that she had been passed over twice for promotions she knew she deserved. She emphasized her words by tapping her extremely long, brightly painted fingernails on the desk. As she complained, she snapped her gum in disgust. She fingered the large gold heart hanging at the neckline of her unkempt, slightly stained blouse before she adjusted her short skirt.

Hmmm. It is not too hard to see what was holding this woman back.

After discussing her professional demands and personal needs, I created a personal Look Book for her. We assembled a workable wardrobe with everything organized for easy matching. We shopped to fill in the wardrobe gaps and to create new, updated looks. We further polished her image with a professional makeover, head to toe. She quickly looked the part of a very professional, promotable leader. The nonverbal message she now sends is very different from before.

You can create your own, individual, personalized Look Book. Collect photographs or sketches of the

(continues)

(continued)

specific looks you really like. The process will sharpen your eye forever, and ideally you will develop an educated, more discriminating, pallet.

The goal of this process is to define the style and image you would like to create and maintain, and specifically what is appropriate right now to your personal and professional demands.

To make your personalized Look Book, have fun. Use your imagination. This is the time to break out of the mold, to do what you have always wanted to do, and be who you want to be. What to do? Define the attitude, the look, the wardrobe pieces, and accessories (scarves, ties, jewelry, eyewear, briefcase, and so on), the posture and stance, the makeup and hair color—everything.

For inspiration, buy European fashion magazines to see future fashion trends, as they are traditionally ahead of the fashion curve. (See it in Paris, Milan, or London today and wear it a couple of years later in the United States.) If you are lucky enough to travel internationally, observe what's happening wherever you are.

Next, and this is the hardest part, evaluate whether or not your choices are flattering, appropriate, the right color and fabric, and a powerful style for you and your daily life demands. Are they great looking and becoming on you? Do they enhance your best features and minimize your challenges? Select silhouettes, colors, styles, trends, classics, accessories, clothes, shoes, hair, glasses, coats, casual to very dressy—the works! It may be that long jackets hide your not-quite-slim waist, while shorter skirts reveal your great legs.

Once you have established the looks you want, go through every single item in your closet and determine if it supports your new image. If it does, rehang it neatly in your closet. If it doesn't, give it away or toss it. Now. Don't leave anything to chance. This is serious work to be done, and done completely now, so you can forget about it and concentrate on the real career work at hand.

Lastly, shop carefully and prudently to fill in those holes.

inexpensive pocket squares.) If you have the funds, go wild over your shoes. Imelda's horde might have been extravagant, but nobody ever accused her of wearing the wrong shoes. Second, buy classic styles. If taken care of, these styles will last you many years, if not a lifetime.

Ellen's Essentials

A lint roller is a must. Use it on all clothing *prior to taking clothing off the hanger just before putting it on.* Then use it during the day as needed. Keep a lint roller with you. Have one at the office. Bring one with you everywhere, especially when you travel. They remove lint, human hair, pet hair, and general debris that attaches instantly and constantly to your clothing, especially on the day of that big presentation. If you don't have a lint roller handy, in a pinch use 2-inch-wide tape, wrapped around your hand, sticky side out.

What clothes should I avoid if I want to look powerful and professional?

Don't be a fashion victim. Avoid clothing that is too revealing, too tight, too unconventional, too trendy, too different, too striped, too bold, too colorful, too too.

Don't wear anything that distracts your audience. Avoid items that dangle, jangle, sparkle, or glitter. Don't wear anything that needs constant adjustment. A great scarf at your neck is a marvelous idea to frame your face and draw attention while looking very professional. Silk is usually the favored fabric for a scarf, however, silk does move and slip, even come untied. Use a beautiful brooch to secure it in place if you want to be free of worry or distraction. Do wear clothing that allows you to move freely.

What colors should I wear for power days versus days I want to be invisible?

All colors have emotional and psychological meanings that influence us whether we realize and acknowledge it or not. Each country, every culture, and even many religious traditions assign different meanings to particular colors. In the United States, these colors have come to have very specific meanings:

- Gem stone colors are full of power and energy. Ruby red, sapphire, and emerald are for days you want to look and feel powerful.

- Pale colors are softer, more childlike. Pink, soft yellow, and baby blue evoke gentler feelings such as compassion and memories of childhood. Wear them on the days you would rather not be noticed, or, if noticed, you want to receive some gentleness and compassion.

- Black is classic, urban, and considered very chic. It is a proper business color and indicates you are all business and know it. It is also the most slenderizing color to wear.

- White was traditionally never worn after Labor Day, but now it can be. White or beige linens are the ultimate summertime look. "Winter white" (wool) is considered to be quite chic. When considering white, any time of the year, understand that it does soil easily and is a stand-out-from-the-crowd color, especially if worn below the waist.

I dressed wrong for the occasion. How can I cover my embarrassment?

If you are fast tracking your career (or want to have a career at all), call ahead and find out what the appropriate attire is. Plan for it. Don't be the odd man or woman out. But if, despite your best efforts, things just don't turn out the way you expected, it's time to regroup.

To overdress or underdress. Ah, that is the question. If you didn't get the word, it is better to overdress than underdress. If you do overdress, remember that you will then have to carry it off gracefully.

Don't *be* embarrassed. After the initial shock, recover ASAP. If you are really disconcerted, go directly to the restroom, stand in a stall, and get a grip on yourself. Give yourself a rousing pep talk and then reappear at the occasion ready to accomplish your goals.

Don't *look* embarrassed. Look and act as if you planned it this way. In fact, you might have had an event immediately prior, or something immediately following this event, with no time to change.

How to pull it off. Hold your head up high, keep your shoulders back, smile broadly, and exude confidence. This way, you will look great and proud in whatever you are wearing. No one will even guess. Be a grand conversationalist and enjoy the occasion.

No excuses. Don't waste time (or lower yourself to) explaining away your outfit, the mistake, miscommunication, misinformation, your embarrassment, your regret, whatever. Don't betray yourself.

Learned your lesson? Do it better next time.

Ellen's Hot Tips

Always Have a Backup Wardrobe

If making an important speech, meeting someone you want to impress, or presenting to your big boss, always have a backup wardrobe, just in case. Better to have it and not use it than to have someone spill their soda or their full buffet plate on you, leaving no time to run home or to buy something. Women should always carry a spare pair of pantyhose for emergencies.

Control the Emotional Climate

How can I be one of those people who has more charisma?

Being charismatic means others want to be around you, they seek you out, and they vie for your attention. Charisma is an energy everyone has inside, and it bubbles out of you to attract others. You have it inside you right now. As you are reading this, your charisma is yearning to come out and play. Charisma is your unique personal style, wit, and charm, combined with your humanity, energy, and soul.

An important part of getting down to business, especially if you want to fast track, is developing or enhancing your charisma. All leaders have it. Think Martin Luther King Jr., the Kennedys, Gandhi, FDR, Winston Churchill, Golda Meir. Many celebrities have it. Think Jackie Onasis, Marilyn Monroe, Mohammed Ali, Lady Diana. You can enhance your own charisma by focusing on the following elements:

- Anticipate and respond to the needs of others.

- Be prepared to act on behalf of the group to solve common concerns, challenges, and problems.

- Be a generous host. Give a gracious "you're welcome" or "my pleasure" when you are thanked. Or a humble "It was nothing."

- Be the person people go to, whether for sports scores or cookies, a laugh or a shoulder to cry on, a pep talk or an honest opinion.

- Enjoy and praise the little things in life.

- See the goodness and the best of everyone's soul.

- Dwell only on the positive.

- Realize the important lessons and values of life. See and appreciate the big picture.

- Be flexible. These days life changes every millisecond. While it's often very difficult to "go with the flow," sometimes it's essential. The bonus: The better you are with change, the more others will flock to you.

I want to be more approachable. How can I do it?

There are myriad ways to adjust your image, attitude, and energy to be approachable. Change the way you dress. Dress more casually. For women, a dress rather than a business suit. For men, a colored shirt rather than white can provide just enough difference to convey an approachable mood. Here are some other ways to help you reach out to others:

- Wear pale colors such as pink. Pink evokes compassion, is nonthreatening, and reminds us subconsciously of helpless, sweet babies.

- Take the opportunity to talk casually with your coworkers.

- Ask someone you don't normally consult for an opinion.

- Invite someone to lunch or coffee.

- Make plans with someone you haven't spent time with.

- Remove your jacket.

- Loosen your tie and unbutton the top button of your shirt.

- Roll up your sleeves. Dress down and loosen up.

Occasionally I want to intimidate. What do you suggest?

There are several elements to intimidation and several ways to intimidate. However, I recommend win-win, teamwork, cooperation, patience, and taking the high road as better alternatives than intimidation in nearly every situation. So please consider the following before you commit to intimidation:

- Why do I want to intimidate someone?

- How do I feel and respond when intimidated?

- Is this the most productive form of behavior for me now?

- Are there alternative methods by which I may achieve my goals? If so, what are they?

- What are the risks to me and to others?

- If my actions were to be printed in the newspaper, would I be proud of myself?

If you're still committed to intimidation, here are some suggestions. Dress more formally in darker, cooler colors. Wear high heels (ladies only, please). Wear new clothes. Wear more sophisticated clothes. Wear high-end makeup (again, for the ladies). Surprise and intimidate others with a new do. Try wearing a bow tie (for both men and women), as they are considered disarming. For women, wear men's clothing: suit, tie, and trousers.

Throw others off guard by changing your behavior. Change boundaries. Change the rules. Keep everyone guessing. Be more remote in everyday conversation. Be extremely brief. Be preoccupied. Maintain silence. Answer

Ellen's Essentials

Ladies, when you discover a "gentleman" staring at your anatomy and making you feel uncomfortable, there is an immediate cure. To gain control of the situation and regain your dignity, stare at *his* anatomy. And I don't mean glance. I mean stare with your eyes, your head, neck, and upper body. With the strongest intent you can muster, *stare*. He will be so intimidated he will stop staring inappropriately and may even flee the scene. (Even nice girls have to fight back sometimes.)

questions with a "Hmmm . . . I will have to get back to you on that." Silence is a master weapon.

I look too young and therefore most people don't give me the credit (responsibility, power, freedom, assistance, money) I deserve. What can I do?

This is a common complaint among my very bright fast-track clients. It often happens on Wall Street. The following tips will be of use to you in reversing the more common I-want-to-look-younger syndrome.

Dress more conservatively than others in your age group. Think of Michael J. Fox on *Family Ties*. He always wore a suit and tie in contrast to both his very casually dressed family and everyone else in his age range. As the audience, we therefore believed him to be the most adult. You can do this, too.

- Buy the best quality you can afford.

- Wear traditional dark colors, grays, pinstripes, small-print ties, pocket squares, cravats.

- Don't wear bold, flashy, or bright clothing.

- Look comfortable in your own skin—understated, elegant, and sophisticated.

Practice excellent manners. You will definitely stand apart from the youth of today.

Grow a beard and/or mustache. Men only, please.

Act older. This means no low-end humor, no excessive hanging out at beer bashes, and no childish pranks. You know the deal. Think mature.

Join professional organizations and be active. Take responsibility. Become an officer, be a leader.

Befriend the veterans. At work and in your field, watch, listen, and learn their mannerisms, habits, and speech. Adopt them for yourself.

Date and marry someone older. Your social circle will then naturally include older people.

Get married. Nothing will add to your credibility more quickly.

Have children. Ditto.

Keep your private life private. Married or not, do not come to work with wild stories of your all-night escapades.

Get season tickets to mature events. Appear at the symphony, the opera, or the ballet, and invite others whom you want to see you as older.

In the end, you may need to demand respect by asking for the money and recognition you deserve.

Use Timing to Your Advantage

I never know when to be early, on time, or fashionably late. How can I know what's appropriate?

It is a fine line. If you're early, you may seem too eager and give the impression you have nothing better to do. If you plan to be late, you may look as though you don't respect other people's time or the agenda. So ask. Timing is every-thing. Get it right.

- If the event is work related, ask your boss, col-leagues, or human resources, who have knowledge and experience of your company's expectations. Follow the mentor.

- If outside of work, arrange to go with someone, preferably someone reliable, who knows the eti-quette and protocol of the group.

- Whether the event is work related or not, consult the meeting or event planner as to what is appro-priate for the particular situation.

If all else fails, arrive early. Check out the situation. If you're obviously too early, make some plausible excuse to

Ellen's Essentials

Personally, I always try to make time to check out a new venue prior to the event scheduled there. Most of the time, it is what I expected. Sometimes, however, it is something completely different, and in these cases, I am more than pleased I took the time to investigate. I am not fond of surprises.

leave (for example, remember that you have to mail a letter or make a phone call). Be sure to confirm the appropriate time to return later.

I feel so awkward the first hour of a meeting or event. What do you recommend so I look and feel more comfortable?

Make that first hour meaningful. Immediately prior to entering, review your Pre-Event Planning Organizer (see page 17) for who you want to see, meet, be seen with, and be seen by. In addition, before any important meeting or event, create your own Private List. Work this list at the event. If you need to review it, go into a private bathroom stall, pull it out of your wallet, and review it. Do not let anyone see it or even know about this secret list. It's private—that's why I call it the "Private List." After the event, review your Private List. Evaluate what you accomplished, what you didn't, and why. Write down the lessons learned so each time you can benefit from your past experience.

No one but you knows you're uncomfortable, until you show them or tell them.

—Ellen A. Kaye

After the party is over, congratulate yourself. Be proud of your commitment. If you accomplished most of the items on your Private List, you are well on your way to creating a powerful, professional leadership image. It will be noticed and rewarded by others. Now give *yourself* a reward for a job well done. You've earned it.

Make Your Private List Count

Ellen's
Checklist

1. Set a personal goal to maximize your time at the event. For example, "I will meet at least five new people, reconnect with three people, and talk with two people I have been avoiding but should speak to about company business."

2. As you enter, survey and assess the situation. Who's Who? To whom are they talking? Why? And Who's Where? Search the room visually for their location.

3. Waste no time in moving in their direction. To maximize your move, go in the direction you think will provide you with the most meeting opportunities in case your first choice has moved or is unavailable to you. Be aware others may be doing the same thing you are doing, so the people you are trying to meet may move before you get to them.

(continues)

(continued)

4. Immediately seek out and address the most senior or highly visible people present. Whether you know them or not, it doesn't matter. You will now. An added bonus: Everyone watching you will assume you do know these famous folks, or they will be in awe of you for your courage and composure.

5. No pain, no gain. Push yourself to be sociable, friendly, and accessible. Mingle. Wind through the room and around the seating, shaking hands and exchanging pleasantries with friends, colleagues, dignitaries, and new faces. Meet and greet as many people as possible.

6. Use the opportunity to meet those you don't know. This is an excellent time to make a first contact with superiors you may not normally have access to.

7. Reconnect with busy people who are never available.

8. Seek out and compliment someone you have admired and not yet had the opportunity to meet.

I've made a great business contact. How do I proceed from here?

Avoid a post-networking nightmare. It's always the same problem. What can you do to distinguish yourself from the masses of other people vying for the limited time and attention of a new business contact? Sure, you can send a note and your business card. However, that's what everyone else is doing. Why not try something different?

Taking photos provides a great excuse to follow-up with someone. Send a "wonderful to meet you/see you again" note and include the photo of the two of you. Framed or unframed, the recipient will be flattered by your thoughtfulness and impressed by your effort.

Traditionally, it is considered rude and unacceptable to include your business card in a personal note such as this. However, your purpose is to develop a professional relationship, so split the difference. Write a quick note with only pleasantries. Separately, include a simple piece of good stationery, folded to the size of the photo and print, "If you would like more copies of this photo, please don't hesitate to call me." Include your name and numbers. *Bon chance!*

Photocopy the picture for your color-coded files. You now have a quick visual reminder of when you contacted that person. Don't forget to write full names, company names, the name of the event at which you met, the date, and business intent.

Ellen's Hot Tips

How to Leave an Event Early Without a Scene

You don't want to be the first to arrive (unless you want to help set up) or the last to leave. If you need to leave early, be courteous and call your host in advance. Explain that you have prior commitments you must attend to and, therefore, must leave at a particular time. Express your apologies and your regret that the conflict is unavoidable.

This way you will not appear rude when you duck out just as the keynote speaker begins or as the dessert is being served. If either looks boring, other guests will envy your forethought.

Frame your copy of the photo and put it in your office for all to see/drool over. You will eventually have a great photo gallery power wall.

At times, I need to be in the spotlight. How can I get attention?

Command it. Demand it. Plan for it. Call for the ball. Specifically, you should consider any or all of the following ways of taking center stage:

- If you think you can complete the deal, ask for the chance.

- Be the one to conduct dialogue among your peers and with your boss.

- Plan a social event for your group. Invite colleagues to lunch.

- Post items of interest (articles, financial advice, vacation spots, or great Web site addresses) on your group's bulletin board.

- Think about the needs of your coworkers and fill the void.

- Dare to be the odd-man-out. If you're voting no, while everyone else is voting yes, explain your reasoning.

- Dress differently: more formally, more casually, more expensively. Change your makeup: the amount you wear, the color palette.

- Change your hair color and cut to surprise everyone Monday morning.

- Throw an office party. Invite your colleagues out for cocktails or coffee, or a special occasion.

- Volunteer to be on the committee (or form one) that celebrates birthdays. With any luck, the person who's on the receiving end will adore you for this.

- Bring in lunch for your group. Treat for doughnuts or bagels in the morning.

- Do excellent work.

Potpourri

Americans are obsessive about cleanliness. What do I need to know with regard to current American hygiene standards?

Americans are taught that to be successful, or even worthy as a person, we must always have mint-fresh breath, no body odor, shiny hair, and straight, white teeth. Whether you perceive such concerns as superficial or monumentally important, the fact is that the people you are trying to persuade *do* think it's important and may reject your message if they perceive you as unhygienic or unkempt.

How you look, dress, and carry yourself is just as critical to establishing rapport and credibility as good content and a powerful introduction. Everything should work together. Every impression counts. Don't let dangling details damage or derail your credibility.

How to Avoid Bad Hair Days

Ellen's Hot Tips

Men tend to have little trouble finding a good haircut. Women, who face an infinite number of styling options, have to work a little harder to find just the right hair colorist, cutter, and stylist. To find the stylist of your dreams, look for women with great cuts and flattering styles, and ask who cut their hair. Where? When?

Start the conversation with an effective and flattering: "Oh, I love your hair. It's exactly the color (cut, style) I have been looking for. Would you mind terribly telling me who does it? I would be so grateful." I can almost guarantee it's the best thing she has heard all day, and she'll be tripping over herself to help you with the information you request.

My hair is a mess. What can I do to be sure it doesn't distract people from hearing my message?

Your hair should always be clean, neat, well cut, and well groomed. Wear it off your face and never touch it, except when styling it in the bathroom. Your hair is the frame for your face, and it is well worth the money to have it professionally cut, colored (if you so choose), and styled. Here's what you should be aware of:

Haircut. I am a big fan of finding a great hair cutter and sticking with a good thing. One good haircut, no matter how much it costs, can make a significant contribution to your rise to power. Think of the personal joy of no more bad hair days. Think of the time you save each day, not to mention the embarrassment, frustration, and those self-defeating negative feelings when you know, deep down, you could look much better, if only . . .

Hair color. If your natural color is not flattering, exciting, or dynamic, or if you just want a change, try something else. Look through magazines and collect photographs of hair colors you like before you go into a salon.

Dandruff. Unsightly and embarrassing, dandruff littered across your clothing is a big distraction and a total turnoff to others. Although you may not see it as you look down at your chest, there may be masses of unsightly spots strewn on your shoulders and back. Right or wrong, dandruff implies you are dirty and gives the impression you are unconscious of, or unconcerned with, how you appear to others.

Ellen's Hot Tips

The Perfect Presentation Test for Dandruff

Do you have it? Whether you think you might have dandruff, or know you don't, take this test every three months or so and confirm reality. Pair it with the first day of every quarter or with something else you will remember.

1. In private, put on a dark jacket and then brush or comb your hair.

2. Now check your shoulders and back area, closely, in the mirror. Do be sure to have your glasses on if you wear them.

3. If you don't see any dandruff, carefully remove your jacket and check the shoulders and back area more closely.

4. If you find nothing, put the jacket on again. Brush or comb your hair again.

5. Check your shoulders and back in about one hour. If you find nothing, good for you. Count yourself blessed.

(continues)

(continued)

6. If you discover dandruff at any point during the test, don't despair. Certainly, don't go into denial, as that will defeat our purpose here. If you have it, admit it, and get rid of it. Besides, everyone else sees it, so you are fooling no one but yourself. Take action and conscientiously try to cure the problem. Here is how to go about it:

- Brush your hair daily, prior to putting your clothes on.

- Wash your hair often to keep it clean and fresh.

- Start a habit of brushing off your shoulders and back area as often as possible (at least every hour). Do this in private or discretely, please.

- Change your hair-care products; sometimes this simple solution is the cure.

- See your dermatologist if the problem persists.

> ■ See a different dermatologist if the first one
> doesn't help you.
>
> There is a cure out there for everyone. Sometimes
> it just takes a bit of time and effort to find it.

I worry about having bad breath and not knowing it. How can I be sure my breath is fresh and clean?

Basic dental care means you brush at least twice a day, floss daily, use mouthwash and mints, have biannual cleanings, and see your dentist on a regular basis. Beyond the basics, here are some other essentials to keep you smiling:

Guard against bad breath, halitosis, malodor. No matter what you call it, bad breath may be tricky. About 75 percent of bad breath starts in the mouth. When oxygen and debris mix in the mouth, they produce sulfur compounds that cause foul odor. Halitosis may simply be caused by something you ate. In addition, many other things can cause bad breath. It may be an indication you have something seriously wrong, such as a sinus infection, gastrointestinal problems, or periodontal disease. It may be an indication of something less serious such as stress, the onset of a cold, or stomach problems.

Avoid dehydration. Dehydration, or dry mouth, can cause bad breath six times faster than a hydrated mouth. Sometimes dehydration is increased by medications such as antidepressants, asthma drugs, antihistamines, some blood pressure medications, and alcohol. So be sure to drink lots of water daily.

Check your own breath. Unfortunately, you may not be aware of your own bad breath while others always are. To check yourself, in private, exhale through your mouth into the cupped palm of your hand and inhale slowly. Note the odor. Or, lick the back of your hand, let it dry, and then smell it. Or try this new way: Use a Halimeter, which measures the amount of sulfur-producing bacteria in your mouth.

Be proactive. See your dentist for checkups and regular cleanings. Brush better, and always brush after meals. Use an electric toothbrush. Rake your tongue. Use floss regularly. Freshen your mouth and breath with mouthwash; use it each time you brush—and even when you don't.

Ellen's Essentials

Always take the mint—and the hint. If someone offers you a mint or a breath freshener, always take it. If he is offering you a subtle hint, don't be offended. Say thanks and be grateful.

Keep breath mints with you at all times. Use and offer them often and freely. Mints are a fast and easy way to freshen up but do not replace brushing. Surprise, surprise! Mints may also be a great conversation opener.

These days everyone seems to have white teeth but me. What do they know that I don't?

In our society, white teeth are a tremendous asset. If your teeth aren't white and bright, go directly to the dentist. Do not pass Go. Plan to spend about $200 to $300. Your dentist can give you treatments to dramatically whiten your teeth. It's easy, painless, and oh so worthwhile. The cost is nominal but the impact is significant.

I think I understand the basics of good hygiene, but what else should I pay attention to when getting ready for a meet and greet?

Once you have mastered the big items—cleanliness, hair style, wardrobe, and bright smile—be sure to pay attention to the rest of the details. Remember, everything about your appearance is important; incorporate these more subtle aspects of good hygiene in your daily routine:

Body odor. Like it or not, somewhere along the line, someone decided natural body odor is not acceptable. So if you are not showering daily and using deodorant or antiperspirant, go directly to the nearest store, buy antiperspirant, and use it daily without fail. The slogan "Never let them see you sweat" has sold millions of cans of deodorant. As *Homo sapiens,* we all have a unique scent originally intended to stimulate sexual attraction, mating, and procreation. However, this is the twenty-first century and antiperspirant sales are skyrocketing.

Unsightly or excessive hair. Men: Always be clean-shaven and/or well-trimmed. Keep weekly tabs on your nose hair, ear hair, and brows. Women: Remove excess hair on your upper lip and everywhere else. Have your brows shaped and trimmed professionally.

This may seem like an unnecessary luxury, but it is not. Once your brows are organized to complement your bone structure, they will be a daily source of good looks.

Nails. Nails should always be spotlessly clean. Men should buy a nailbrush and scrub under nails daily, or more often when necessary. Women must have well-manicured nails. Use pale polish in a conservative workplace; darker colors may be permissible in a more liberal environment. Moderate lengths (a quarter-inch beyond the fingertip) are the only way to go in a professional atmosphere. Nothing longer, and no sparkles, no glitter, no decorative decals.

Makeup. Your makeup should enhance your look, not distract from it. If you are going on television, or when your image is to be projected on a large screen, use a foundation or a base with good coverage to even out your skin tones, an under-eye concealer, powder to prevent shine, and lip gloss. The lights will wash out the colors in your face and put big shadows under your eyes and nose. Use just a little makeup to be sure your projected image is what you want it to be. If you have a receding hairline, your forehead may shine. A little bit of powder will keep the lights from flaring up.

Miscellaneous critical details. Everything should be buttoned properly. Make sure your zipper is up and locked. Check to see that your shirt is tucked in and your hemline is straight. Missing these small details can derail your credibility and be endlessly embarrassing.

Mirror. Carry a compact and give yourself a quick and discreet once-over regularly. Make sure you don't have anything on your face, in your teeth, on your nose, or in the corners of your eyes.

Ellen's Believe It or Not

A senior vice-president in an international accounting firm retained me to work separately with two of his brilliant mid-level executives. At our initial meeting, one executive arrived with coffee stains on his tie, mismatched clothing, hair looking unwashed for weeks, and dirty fingernails. In tight competition for my attention were his open fly and his short socks, both of which made me privy to far too much information. When asked about his appearance, he said all that mattered was the quality of his work.

Working with me, he realized his slovenly appearance communicated to his company and his clients sloppy work habits and lack of attention to detail.

We started with the basics: good personal hygiene; clean, matching, well-fitted, pressed clothing; and zipper up. I worked on his wardrobe, preparing specific outfits for him and eliminating the guesswork. He is now well groomed and looks professional.

This executive confided, "What's very cool is colleagues and clients are treating me with more respect. Who knew! Although I was dead-set against it at first, I get so many compliments that I can't ignore the facts. I'm proud of the way I look now."

I'm sitting at my desk. What can I do to look professional and hard at work?

Some things can't be faked. For starters, really *be* professional and *be* hard at work. Organize your desktop and work hard—a no-brainer! If that won't work for you at the moment, you can stumble into it with little effort. Think about what you need to accomplish for the day. Make a short list. Plan the most efficient way to get it done. File and clear away what you don't need for the task. Arrange the items you do need.

Thinking, planning, and arranging will look quite impressive. So will doing business over the phone. Before long, and quite by accident, you will look professional and be hard at work working. Put aside the coffee, loosen your tie, and try really working. It may come more easily than you thought.

If you are in a meditative state and need "think time," close your door; otherwise you do look bad. Right or wrong, sitting gazing into space does look as though you aren't working, even though creative breakthroughs sometimes come from these moments.

How do I get rid of my nervous habits? I want to make a good impression.

Don't think you are alone. Almost everyone needs to let go of one nervous habit or another. It can be a "catch 22" if one of the reasons you have a nervous habit is all the pressure not to be nervous! Isn't life grand! So many little ironies.

Recognizing you have nervous habits is half the challenge. Many people are blind to their nervous habits, or in denial. The problem with this is that everyone else sees them. You should, too. Don't be the last to know. Watch yourself on video. Sometimes that's enough to get you on the path to self-correction. For example, a former client was playing with her pen, clicking it over and over. When

I asked if she was nervous, she said "No." Asked if she was aware she was constantly clicking her pen, she said "No." Once she was made aware of it, she said she was doing it "because it feels so good, not because I'm nervous."

Reality check: When a useless, repetitive action or motion feels good, it is because you are nervous (or going unconscious) and your autonomic nervous system has taken over. Remember to stay conscious. Hold your hands and body still until you consciously choose to move a specific part of your body for a specific task.

Here are a few ideas to help you get control of or rid yourself of your nervous habits:

Work out. Do yoga. Play competitive sports. Swim. Take dance lessons. Meditate.

Try a reflexologist. They can be amazingly insightful and solve the problem very quickly.

Don't hesitate to see a therapist. Whether they admit it to you or not, lots of very influential people have done just that. Good therapy is worth its weight in gold. Consider it a personal and professional investment.

See a doctor. If you are feeling unmotivated, lethargic, or depressed, ask your doctor to check you out. Discover the problem and cure it. If medication will help, give it a try. Don't waste time with indignation, self-righteousness, fear, or shame. There is so much going on in the world right now that we sometimes put ourselves last, suffering needlessly. Take care of yourself.

I never look good in photographs and our corporate portrait is coming up. Any ideas on how I can look good?

Top executives worldwide ask me this question. Here is my secret scoop on how to maximize this photo op:

Check out the company's previous photographs. Observe carefully the clothing, body and head positions, posture, angle of the body and head to the camera, position of the arms and hands. A little study goes a long way. Look in magazines, books, and newspapers to see what you think looks good and what you want captured for posterity.

Pretend your mirror is the camera and practice positions so you can re-create them from physical memory. After modeling and acting for years, take it from me: Almost nothing that looks good on camera ever feels natural. So practice. Try several expressions and positions.

Think of someone or something that makes you happy, proud, or confident. Whatever the look you want, create an emotional memory or musical trigger

Ellen's Essentials

A very handsome senior vice president in the aeronautics industry complained to me that he always looked terrible in pictures. Building security required he always wear a photo ID. He looked like a "Most Wanted" fugitive, and he asked me for help. Since I knew thoughts of his daughter always brought a sparkle to his eye, I suggested that each time he looks into the camera he think of his darling daughter. He did. Now he gets compliments on his ID photo all the time.

for that look. Recall it before and during the photo session, as you look directly into the camera lens. This is a very powerful technique.

Someone I trusted let me down. How can I prevent this in the future?

Prevent future problems by appointing yourself the "Deal Shepherd," and see everything through to completion. How much time, money, prestige, production, and commission is this worth to you? If your answer is "a lot," take full responsibility for each and every step of the deal. Here is how to go about it:

Rethink and redefine your responsibility in the deal. If you've been pushing off your responsibilities on subordinates or colleagues, remember who it is that actually stands to lose if the deal falls through. If it's you, take charge.

Beware of the "Slip Through the Cracks" syndrome. As the official Deal Shepherd, establish the agenda. Set deadlines. Establish milestones. Require confirmation. Stay on it. Agree in writing. Follow up in writing. Confirm in writing.

> *When you delegate, don't abdicate.*
>
> —*David Lewis Blackwell*

If a milestone is missed, take action. The Deal Shepherd stays on top of small deadlines to ensure that major deadlines are met.

Be a "Doubting Thomas." Ask for concrete evidence that deadlines are being met. Review preliminary drafts. Inspect progress. Oversee training. Ask for statements, receipts, and other supporting documents.

Chapter 2

CONVERSATIONS

- Put Your Best Self Forward
- Giving Voice to Your Message
- Talking with Clients
- Interacting with Coworkers
- The Art of Listening
- Phone Talk
- Potpourri

CONVERSATION MAY NOT BE A LOST ART, BUT
effective conversationalists have certainly been on the wane
in recent years. The more we speed up our lives, the less we
seem to take in as we go whizzing by. Business is rarely car-
ried on at a leisurely pace, yet the underlying principles of
good conversation still serve us well. You are more likely
to get what you want—a raise, a big order from a client

company, the appreciation of your coworkers—if you polish your conversational skills. It doesn't take any longer to be polite and considerate with others, and you will find that it pays huge dividends, if not this minute, at some future time. Pay attention to what you are saying—and *how* you are saying it. Is your approach getting you what you want? If not, try some of the strategies from this chapter and learn to talk the "good talk."

Put Your Best Self Forward

I'm new and I'm shy. How do I talk to people?

Newness is a temporary problem. The how and when of talking to new people is, of course, a matter of personal style. A great many people fear speaking to groups, or even individuals, especially before they know them well. Perhaps you typically need a little extra time to adjust. Take it. If you are worried about being accepted, wait and join the group slowly. But don't wait too long. Now here are some specific things to do to fit into the group:

- Say hello when you see your colleagues.

- Ask if you can lend support.

- Help finish a task.

- Take chances.

- Get involved.

- Pay a compliment.

- Ask a related question. Ask an unrelated question.

- Ask someone for help. "Would you mind giving me some advice?"

- Share something. "Did you hear _____?"

- If you get shot down, laugh it off, and try, try again.

You won't be new or shy for long if you practice these strategies. Talking to other people will soon become easy and natural for you.

People think I am arrogant, but I really just feel awkward in conversation. How can I change this perception?

You've had an interesting insight about yourself. Your awkwardness is perceived as arrogance because you hold back or keep your distance. You seem remote and uninvolved because you don't venture much, and when you do, it is perhaps abrupt.

The solution is to listen and learn. Open up more. Put aside your need to be safe for the moment. Show you are friendly and approachable. Invite a coworker to lunch or some other casual activity. Choose a colleague or two to befriend. People's perception of you as arrogant will evaporate as you demonstrate openness and approachability.

My boss said I need to be more diplomatic. What does that mean, and how can I do it?

There's a way to say everything that needs to be said. Diplomacy is that way. It means taking the high road— whether you are talking casually with a colleague or client, making a sale, or negotiating the future of Microsoft.

It takes careful listening and insightful observation to become a diplomat, but it's a skill you can develop. Here are the essentials:

Study people. Study what motivates the people you are working with. Is your colleague eager for recognition or afraid of the spotlight? Is he or she in need of help in an area of expertise? Is your potential client looking to shine or just performing routinely to rigid corporate standards? Are the goals conceptual or concrete? Is the current deal based on speed of delivery, quality, price, or value? What else? What motivates these people?

Learn the client's business model or your colleague's way of working. Knowing the process will allow you to facilitate it. That's the political side. You can expect someone to do only what's appropriate within his or her system. You can offer to solve a problem in your client's system with the way you do business.

Add value. Beyond the basics, what subtle value added will allow you to propose a much better deal for all involved?

Understand your own business. Understand clearly your own goals and the ways in which your business works best. Where does your profit or advancement actually come from? Which typical client demands are easy to provide? Which are difficult?

Acknowledge the client's needs and state your own. By acknowledging their needs, you pave the way for them to acknowledge yours.

Prepare ways to say "no." A blunt "no" may eventually be necessary, but a counteroffer is even better. You and your company need to grow from this transaction. Offer what you can in lieu of refusing what you can't.

Leave everyone with options. Make sure they have a chance to win something as well. In business, you must honor everyone's need to succeed, profit, and live to do another deal.

Once you understand what both sides need, and how they work, you are prepared to be a diplomat. Part of diplomacy is maintaining the delicate balance of your interest and theirs—over time. What will you deliver this time, and what will you deliver in the future? What will you get this time, and what will you get in the future? Far better to have a relationship that works over time than to go for the kill in the first contract. The sooner you develop lasting profitable relationships, the sooner you'll get to the golf course or spa.

I've got good news! How do I announce it to my boss?

When you have good news, you need to take advantage of the opportunity. Delivering the news to your boss, if done correctly, can help you fast track your career.

Prepare a memo with the good news. Memorializing information saves a record for posterity, establishes the date and time, and permanently associates it with you. As always, be concise.

Deliver the news, with the memo in hand, in person. You want to train your boss to associate good news with your face. "Sabin Company tripled the size of their contract with us; I wrote up the details for your review." Do this sooner rather than later so *your* news remains *yours*.

Can I use humor in a tense situation without looking foolish?

Yes, no, and maybe. Granted, everyone loves to laugh. Using humor, however, is a big, *big* risk, even for professional comedians. Think about how many years Jay Leno, Bill Cosby, Rita Rudner, Steve Martin, David Letterman, and other comedians have worked and worked honing their craft—making each joke perfect, preparing each setup, layering, creating tiebacks, and being consistently funny. And each one of these folks is very bright and surely gifted with a quick wit from birth.

If your humor works, you're an ace. You break the tension, giving everyone a chance to laugh and regroup. They love you. They want you around. You're a star. If, perchance, your humor doesn't work, you have exponentially escalated a tense situation into an even tenser situation.

Having said all this, choosing to use humor really depends on each situation. Use these guidelines to help you make your decision:

Yes. If you are really funny, sure of yourself, and have no doubt whatsoever that everyone else in this tense situation will enjoy and appreciate your humor, go, Slugger!

Maybe. Answer the following questions honestly.

- Have you ever been described as funny?

- Do people generally hang out with you because they think you are funny?

- Are you a good joke teller?

- Are you great at pointing out the humor in any given situation and having everyone crack up?

If you can't answer these questions in the affirmative, the answer is probably "no." With all due respect, you may be the next Jim Carrey. (If you are, by the way, contact me ASAP because I would love your help making my next book funnier.)

No. If there's even the remotest chance you're not great at ad-lib humor, I strongly recommend you play it straight and leave the jokes to the office cutup.

Giving Voice to Your Message

How can I make my voice sound more authoritative?

There are many creative ways to work with your voice to sound more authoritative. Most people don't know what their voices sound like, so start to familiarize yourself with the range, inflection, variety, and power of your own voice. Play with lowering your voice an octave. Focus your attention and place your voice deeper in your body, in your diaphragm rather than your throat. Here are some other tips:

- Listen to other voices. Start to recognize what makes a voice sound authoritative.

- Listen to mothers, fathers, teachers, and coaches reprimanding or vocalizing authority. Emulate that.

- Open your mouth wide when you speak.

- Don't mumble. Enunciate clearly.

- Project your voice. Always speak to the back of the house.

Ellen's Hot Tips

Develop Your Authoritative Voice

This exercise helps you to calm your system, concentrate, and place your voice where it is strongest and most authoritative:

- Put your hand on your belly. This is where your voice should come from.

(continues)

(continued)

- Feel your belly expand when you inhale and contract when you exhale. Repeat this twelve times, slowly, concentrating on filling and emptying your belly.

- Now start vocalizing. This means saying vowels *a, e, i, o,* and *u* as you exhale. Mentally place your voice in your belly under your hand. Go through the vowels several times, speaking on the exhale.

- Be aware of what this feels like. Remember it.

When you return to regular speech, recall the feeling you had during this exercise. Speak from this same, deep place. Remember the sense of calm and power of your deep voice. Go impress the world!

I want to be more articulate. What can I do?

There are a multitude of powerful ways to become more articulate. Here are several solid suggestions to get you started:

- Think before you speak.

- Don't mumble. Enunciate clearly. Pronounce each word completely.

- Be literate. Read the classics, Shakespeare, poetry. Join a book club. Take a writing class.

- Develop your vocabulary. Learn five new words a day and use them. Play scrabble. Do crossword puzzles. Join a debating club.

- Learn other languages. Learn Latin.

- Develop a circle with whom you have conversations—not merely daily task sorts of conversations, but cogent discussions about real topics: literature, art, music.

- Seek out others who have a more extensive vocabulary than you do. This will give you a chance to learn and practice.

- Pronounce all words correctly. Watch out for: *Across,* not "accrost." *Asked,* not "axed." *February,* not "Febuary." *Nuclear,* not "nucular." *Often,* not "off ten." *Ostensibly,* not "ostensively." *Peremptory,* not "preemptory." *Sherbet,* not "sherbert." *Supposedly,* not "supposably." Suite of rooms, suit of clothes.

- Try to resist using slang, regionalisms, folksy expressions, and street language. This means no more "wazzup," "hey," "yo," "like," "awesome," or "totally" anything.

How can I make my voice more powerful?

Do the following exercise religiously and your voice will be much more powerful in no time.

Breathing and voice placement. Most Americans, especially women, speak from their throats. If you have ever had laryngitis, you are clearly a throat speaker. The goal is to speak from your diaphragm. This gives you the most power, vocal flexibility, and vocal longevity. Put your hand on your belly. Take several slow, long deep breaths. Feel your stomach expand as you inhale and contract as you exhale. Place your voice under your hand. Speak from there.

Always speak on the exhale. Take a deep breath and speak as you exhale, then you will have enough air to last throughout your sentence.

Read children's storybooks aloud. Become each character and develop a different voice, tone, pacing, pitch, and passion for each character. This is a very effective way to train yourself to speak more powerfully, with more inflection and expression. This can have a tremendous impact on your vocal strength in a very short time with just a little practice. Another benefit is that you will be more interesting to listen to, so people will listen to you more often and for longer periods of time. Speaking will be more fun and less effort for you.

Read the phone book aloud and make it interesting for your listener. This is a classic acting exercise to work on one's voice. Assign a different emotional attitude toward each group of six names, numbers, and addresses. Tape yourself and then listen to the tape. Do you sound interesting? You should. The great challenge of this exercise is to show you that speaking is *not* about the words. It is not about the names, or numbers, or even about the context. It's the energy, tone, pacing, pauses, and punch that make the difference in whether something is interesting or not.

Start paying attention to trained, professional voices. Listen to politicians, speakers, and actors on television, on the radio, in the movies, and at the theater. These people must use their voices constantly. Emulate them. Become aware of the vast variety of vocal patterns and powers.

Cartoon voices are another rich source of vocal variety. Watch Saturday morning television to stimulate your creativity. Play with your voice. Experiment. Mimic other voices. Create your own new and innovative voices. Imitate cartoon character voices. Practice, play, and make children giggle. This will prove you are really into it; kids are a tough and honest audience.

Speak to the back of the house. This is a rule of thumb for actors performing in a theater. Place your focus on speaking to someone at the very back wall, the farthest spot in the room. It is amazing how much this technique really works.

Last time I gave a speech, I got nervous and suddenly lost my voice. How can I prevent this next time?

I call this "preperformance laryngitis syndrome." Don't worry. I have a great cure for this. This loss of voice is merely a *symptom* of your nerves acting up. You are so nervous that your vocal cords tighten. Poor little things, they constrict and close your throat. You lose your voice, start to panic, and your vocal cords get tighter. An ugly cycle is in progress.

To loosen your throat and regain your voice, here's the solution. Try it. It really works and feels good, too.

Go somewhere private. Even a bathroom stall will work. At worst, find a corner and turn your back to the crowd. Repeat this affirmation, or something else to calm yourself down: "My full voice flows effortlessly and will fill the room with ease."

Now sit or stand, whichever feels better. Start by placing your fingers behind your head at the base of your neck. Move your fingertips slowly in a rotating motion. Begin with light pressure and press harder as your muscles relax. Continue the massage upward to the place where your neck meets your skull.

Next, massage down your neck to the place where your neck meets your incredibly painful, inhumanly tight shoulders. Place your thumb and forefinger about 2 or 3 inches apart and squeeze your muscles together, hold briefly, then release.

Gently massage around to the sides of your neck. This area may surprise you. It will probably be tight and very painful. Massage gently.

Next, move forward to massage the front of your neck. Go lightly here. Stop before you get to your Adam's Apple. If you need to swallow, you may want to lift your hands completely off the neck.

Place your thumbs up under your chin bone, starting under your ears and massaging forward. Don't be afraid to dig in a little. This will release tremendous amounts of tension.

Finally, let your jaw go slack. Place your fingertips parallel to your jawbone, over the place where your upper and lower jaws connect. Massage until you feel your jaws relax.

Now your vocal cords should be relaxed and your voice restored.

When I get nervous I talk too fast. How can I fix this?

Hmmm . . . let's get a clearer picture of you. As you find yourself looking out at the faces in your audience, do you feel your internal engines revving up to fourth gear? When you start to speak, do you sound as if you are competing for the title of the world's fastest speed talker? And winning? Once those nerves take over, fast talkers talk faster.

Talking too fast is a bad habit. You are sabotaging your success. You're risking the dreaded, mortally wounding, completely embarrassing "Huh?" syndrome, where everyone misses the next part of your speech. You're distracted, your audience loses the impact of your message, and everyone feels cheated, confused, and unsettled.

If talking too quickly is a problem for you or for your audience, the solution is practice. Give your speech in front of the mirror. Tape yourself. Rehearse your material so thoroughly that nerves can't get the best of you. You've done all the work of thinking, creating, and writing your speech; speaking slowly so your audience can understand you deserves at least as much effort.

Slowing Down Fast Talkers

Ellen's Hot Tips

1. **Practice slowing yourself down.** Recondition yourself. Take a deep breath before each sentence, instead of hardly breathing. Enunciate each word clearly. As you speak, allow your listeners time to hear what you are saying and process it. Look into the eyes of the audience to make sure they are with you. If not, slow down even more.

2. **Designate a friend in the audience to give you a prearranged signal every time you need to slow down.** Then remember to look at your companion often and heed the signal. (By the end of your talk, you'll probably hate your one-time friend. It's the old "kill the messenger" deal.) Make sure you have full view of that friend when the seats are full and the house lights are down. The signal may be as simple as holding up a forefinger, or it might consist of holding up a small red piece of paper at head level.

(continues)

(continued)

3. **Write "Slow Down" on the corner, top, and sides of every page of your notes.** Yes, it is hard to believe people pay me a fortune for this very basic advice. But they excel big time, so it's worth every penny.

4. **When you are rehearsing, always rehearse aloud, slowly.** It is vital to get accustomed to hearing yourself actually speak the words slowly. Consciously slow down. Get used to hearing yourself speak more slowly. When you are "on" you will naturally speed up, so in rehearsal allow for that.

Remember, if you have a tendency to speak too fast, you are probably going the right speed if you feel as if you are going too slowly.

It seems that I am always being asked to repeat myself. How can I be heard the first time?

If you mumble, even friends who want to hear what you have to say may not ask you to repeat yourself. You may be tired, out of sorts, underpaid, overworked, stressed out,

Evaluate Your Speech Pattern

If you answer "yes" to any of the following questions, you may have developed the habit of mumbling. Fortunately, you have the opportunity, right now, to begin your road to recovery. Whatever the reason you started mumbling, it's time to lose the habit.

Yes	No	
_____	_____	Are you afraid to say what you really want to say?
_____	_____	Are you fearful of being misunderstood?
_____	_____	Were you told as a child to "be seen and not heard"?
_____	_____	Are you sometimes uncertain of how to say what you want to say?
_____	_____	Do you feel scared of how what you say will be received?
_____	_____	Do you ever feel stupid or insecure?
_____	_____	Once you start your sentence, do you wish you'd kept your mouth shut?
_____	_____	Are you afraid of failure?
_____	_____	Do you think you have low self-esteem?
_____	_____	Do people often ask you to repeat yourself?

under pressure, or having a bad hair day. I recently had a new client try to explain away his mumbling by saying he didn't want to "scare me off" with his "big voice." Whatever your reason for mumbling, get past it. It's a very sloppy, inconsiderate, and self-defeating habit. Use the checklist on page 93 to evaluate your speech pattern. Then get busy making improvements. Practice speaking clearly and precisely with enough volume to carry your voice to listeners across the room. A clipped accent might feel a bit awkward as you begin your journey out of mumbling, but it will be a relief to your listeners.

Talking with Clients

How do I create rapport with a client?

Creating rapport is a fine art. Master it, and you'll rule the world. Your goal is to diminish the distance between you and your client. Rapport is simply the bridge from one person to another. Try to discover that magic bridge as soon as possible. Here are some suggestions.

> **Find out, in advance, as much as possible about the client.** Ask your predecessor for insights about the client. Call someone who might know this person well. Ask about the client's values, needs, priori-

ties, and passions. Learn what her blind spots are. Uncover her interests, hobbies, and views on life. The more you know about her, the sooner you can give her what she wants. Focus on what is important to the client.

Clear your mind for the introduction and repeat the person's name aloud. Some of you are already ahead of me on this one. Use the person's name three times in conversation as soon as possible. If you meet several people in rapid succession, take the earliest moment to reengage each one, confirm their names, and repeat them to aid memory. Remember, each new acquaintance is valuable to you. Express your pleasure in meeting each one.

Names. Don't be afraid to ask people for their names again or to choose a person among the new acquaintances to help you gain basic information about the others. Ask for a business card, if appropriate. Confirm names, titles, and duties. Honesty and interest will be rewarded, and your willingness to make sincere contact will be impressive.

Courtesy. Respect the client's time and say so. Let the client confirm the scope and length of the conversation. "Debbie and Gracelyn, how much time do you have for me today?"

Eye contact. Make eye contact and show genuine interest in the person you are meeting.

Clarify your relationship and responsibility. "Tommy, I'm the new account executive for your division."

Express your feelings. "Claire, I'm eager to understand and serve your needs."

As you listen, ask questions. At appropriate times, and with the clear purpose of understanding the issues, ask questions. Define cloudy issues. "Joyce, would you kindly explain that further. I'm not completely sure I am following you."

Enter the personal realm if and when the time is right. Look at the environment for clues to personal interests. If a mug on Jack's desk says "coach," you're safe asking, "Are you a coach?" If the response invites further conversation, continue with questions to elicit more information.

Remember the details of the conversation and keep careful notes. Use the tieback technique. Utilize some of the information you gathered earlier in a conversation and ask your client about it. People will be flattered that you remembered and asked. It's an impressive technique.

What do I talk about with a new client?

The client's needs, of course. Ask questions, and try to understand your client's goals and needs. Have a discussion about how you can solve his or her problems. This will solve your conversation dilemma and win your client's confidence.

Interacting with Coworkers

How do I give a compliment without sounding like I'm sucking up?

First, don't save your compliments for the boss—spread them around. When your colleagues and subordinates get plenty of compliments from you, it won't seem out of character for you to compliment clients and supervisors as well.

When complimenting someone from whom you might be seeking approval or favors, be straightforward. Here's the key:

- Be sincere.

- Don't say it unless you mean it.

- Say it in private if you think others will think you are just "sucking up."

- Keep it simple and specific.

- Say it once—or twice, depending on the situation.

What can we do if coworkers have completely different verbal styles?

Work individually and together at bridging the gap, exploring the options, and meeting somewhere in the middle. Let's examine the most common frustration—the one that arises when a Type A personality has to interact with a Type B.

Type A: You talk quickly. You're impatient. You interrupt people and finish their sentences—in a good way, you think. You love knowing what others are going to say and saying it for them. To you, it means you are both on the same page. In fact, you suspect the world would be a better place if everyone else spoke this way, too.

Type B: You talk slowly. You're patient. You let others process through at their own speed while you enjoy the silences. You calmly wish everyone would go a little more slowly and smell the roses.

The result? Both of you are always frustrated; one with the slow speech and endless silence, the other by being chronically interrupted. Try some of these ideas to smooth the flow of conversation. You may be surprised at the results.

Type A: Try a new listening technique. If you can be patient enough to slow down and listen, or if your coworker forces you to listen, you may discover he has some brilliant things to say. In all fairness, slow down. Your colleague has something to contribute. Try to find the triggers that invite open conversation sooner and faster. You'll both benefit.

Type B: Be more forceful. Take responsibility for stating your needs up front. Even thought it is very difficult, seemingly impossible for you, demand your colleague's attention. You'll get a lot of respect in return. Try to give your conclusions first—the details may not matter. Don't be fearful about speaking up. It doesn't have to be perfect—really!

When being introduced to several important senior staff members, my name is mispronounced. Should I say something?

This is always an awkward situation. If you have an uncommon name, one that is difficult to pronounce, or one that is pronounced differently than it is spelled, you'll run into this all the time. If you say something, you risk embarrassing your introducer. If you don't say anything, all the people you have just been introduced to will mispronounce your name. Eventually, when they find out, they, too, will be embarrassed.

When is the best time to correct someone if he mispronounces your name? The very first time he mispronounces it. Your goal is to make it easy for others to remember your name and greet you easily. Watch others' reactions when they are introduced to you. If someone does not get your name, repeat it slowly, spell it slowly, and then repeat it again.

How can you take the sting out? Smile, be casual, and gently speak up. "Oh, people mispronounce my name all the time. It's actually pronounced 'Ziscerigan.'" If you have any helpful hints on how to pronounce your name, or how to remember how to pronounce it, offer them now. "My name rhymes with 'Miss Harrigan.'" If appropriate, tell the history or meaning of your name.

In the end, if your name is really difficult for others to pronounce, you may want to use a nickname or your first name alone. "Yes, I know it is a difficult name to pronounce, so most of my friends just call me Joan. Does that work for you?" This is an easy way around an awkward situation and a good bonding technique as well because you have just created a rapport with this new acquaintance.

If you are the one who can't seem to pronounce the other person's name correctly, use the same hints. Ask

Ellen's Believe It or Not

One of my clients absolutely refused to help people pronounce his difficult name. He felt they should be able to pronounce it properly immediately on their own if they wanted to speak to him. He seriously alienated many people, creating a negative beginning to most relationships. Once he understood the impact he was having on others, he became much more flexible—and likeable.

people questions about their name to show you want to get it right. Everyone will be flattered and impressed that you care enough to take the time and make a point of getting a name correct.

My coworker just told a painfully bad joke. How can I rescue him?

If he makes a habit of it, you have permission to secretly enjoy his pain. If you are a better teller of jokes, tell a brief one, right away.

If you can't remember a joke to save your life, gracefully change the subject. Offer your guests coffee or tea. Praise the view from the conference room window. Ask how the foliage is in Connecticut, even if you're in Dallas in January.

My coworkers walk right past my office. How do I get them to feel welcome to come in?

There are lots of techniques for welcoming people into your zone. Here are some of the best:

To get attention, give attention. If you want others to think of you whenever they're planning something, don't isolate yourself. Get out there and mingle. Make connections. Stop by your colleagues' offices and start conversations. Practice your conversational skills.

Be where the action is. Wherever you are, create the action. Organize events to get the ball rolling. Be the gracious host, the one who always thinks of everything.

Make your office the meeting place. Suggest your office as a place for everyone to meet before going out to lunch, to a staff meeting, or for cocktails after work. This is an easy way for you to let everyone know where your office is and get everyone accustomed to coming by without being obvious.

What goes around, comes around. Once you create some common bonds between you and your colleagues, they will want to stop by your office, keep you posted on office in-

formation, invite you to business events, and even social-
ize outside the office.

Welcome People with Sweets

Ellen's
Hot Tips

Fill a clear (so everyone can see all
the goodies inside) glass or crystal
bowl with bite-size, individually
wrapped candy. Place it on your
desk in clear view from the hallway or door. Every
passerby will be tempted. Some will be brave
enough to stop by, chat, and then ask, "By the way,
may I have one?" You then respond happily and
graciously, "Yes, of course, that's what they are there
for. Please, take two." If you need an excuse to do
this, choose (or create) a holiday or joyous occasion. Anything will do from the obvious (Hal-
loween, Easter, Christmas) to the more esoteric
(your birthday, your first paycheck, you bought a
new car, you got a new account, you have a new
boss, you got a new pet, you won a round of golf or
your bowling league's semifinals).

Be on the alert to passerby, and call people in if
they are too shy or reticent to walk in on their
own, "Hey Tom, come on in for a minute." Tom

(continues)

(continued)

cautiously enters. "Tom, I just wanted to chat. Got a minute? Come on in have a seat. These M&Ms are really good (hold up the bowl to tempt Tom, the unfriendly rascal, until he takes at least one tasty treat). Have a small bowl or ashtray with a crinkled wrapper in it already. This relieves the visitor of the awkward preoccupation and concern over what to do with the used wrappers. Always offer one for the road. People will appreciate you and spread the word.

Variations on a theme: Make a note of who likes what and give them a box of that for the holidays, helping you on a big project, or passing you insider information.

I've got good news! How do I announce it?

Go for the glory when your news is good. Too often, the news is bad. So take full advantage of this opportunity to spread some happiness.

Announce good news to colleagues who worked together on the project. Make a point to get to your coworkers immediately and thank them appropriately. Be sure to give credit where credit is due. In teamwork, giving the entire *team* appropriate credit for the work is what it's all about. Feel great and share the glory.

Announce good news to other coworkers. Fill the break room with treats, but no announcement. Let coworkers ask. Only then do you share the reason. As stated, be brief. After this, you won't have to toot your own horn. In fact, this is the one and only time to be grateful for office gossip and the remarkable speed at which it travels. Trust me, the news will spread like wildfire. Enjoy the heat.

Machiavelli would adamantly disagree, of course. For a very funny, bone-chilling review of Machiavelli's MO, read *What Would Machiavelli Do?* by Stanley Bing. Although it is diametrically opposed to my personal and professional win-win, give credit where it is due philosophy, Bing's dry wit is marvelous, and the prevalence of Machiavellian thought in today's world is made abundantly clear. Read it, weep, and do the opposite.

I'm so low on the totem pole. How can I get the receptionist to take care of me?

Sincere thanks for a job well done is usually helpful. If that doesn't get you anywhere, try excessive flattery. Spa days. Candy. Gifts. Gym passes. Loan of your car when his or hers is in shop. Spare theater tickets.

My coworker talks really quietly.
How can I get this person to speak up?

Talk to your colleague in private. Explain that you would like to hear what she has to say and that it is often difficult to hear her. Ask her to make a conscientious effort to speak louder. Explain that you would be very grateful and it would save you both some embarrassment. Try to help her understand it is advantageous for her to speak louder and be heard.

As another tactic, tell your colleague that you are interested in hearing what he has to say so that you can understand and work as a team. Clearly state that his viewpoint is important to you but that you often have difficulty hearing him. Explain that you understand it is probably you. In fact, say you are sure it is you because your entire family on your father's side, and your mother's side for that matter, and your father's best friend's sister's family is deaf and you clearly may be going deaf. However, regardless of fault, and before you go out to buy that really expensive hearing aid you have been saving up for, you would very much appreciate it if he would try to speak a little louder.

I'm feeling defensive. What can I do
to regain control?

Defensiveness in a business setting can hurt you badly. Above all, you need to exercise control—not control of the situation, mind you, but self-control.

Don't "lose it" by defending your mistake. The worst response to an accusation is to defend what you said, or did, with irrelevant and repetitive explanations. Right or wrong, your boss will see you struggling to cope; your coworkers will lose respect; and worse, you won't admire yourself in the morning.

If you've said or done the wrong thing, take responsibility for it. Ask for guidance and explanation. If you missed the boat, get on board. Adapt quickly. Don't dwell on what you did wrong, but find out what was needed. Even better, find out what is needed now. Do it now. That's evolving for survival.

If you haven't done anything wrong, and you're being wrongly accused, be still. High-pitched, strident denials make you look guilty. Listen quietly to the allegations and wait until your accuser is completely finished speaking. Pause for at least 5 seconds to be sure your accuser is done, and then respond calmly and slowly with a correction. Avoid personal accusations. "Actually, it seems someone gave you incorrect information" or "It appears there's been a glitch in communication" is better than "You've got it totally wrong."

When the situation is resolved—for better or worse—move along. Don't dwell on the negative.

I disagree. How can I argue my point?

With tact, of course, and with a full understanding of the other point of view. Before you plunge in, ask yourself these questions:

- Is this worth putting my career at risk? Whether you're disagreeing with a colleague, a supervisor, or a client, consider whether or not arguing the point might haunt you in the future.

- How much resistance have I already met?

- How much does my opinion matter right now?

- Is it just ego? In business, decisions aren't about you. If it's only your ego crying out to be heard, keep your opinion to yourself.

- Is my argument relevant? Stick to the issues.

- Am I in control of myself? Have the confidence to give your opinion calmly.

If you believe the other person needs to rethink his position, and he has seniority over you, try these strategies.

You are humble and eager to learn. Ask the person with whom you're having a disagreement to explain the decision or conclusion for your benefit. If the explanation is convincing, you've learned something—and avoided painful time on the rack. Say "thank you" to the person.

If you're not entirely convinced, ask for further explanation. If the explanation has a flaw, it'll soon be apparent, and you won't have put the other person on the spot. Wait until you leave the room to pat yourself on the back.

If you don't reach an agreement, you still need to fully understand the other side. Respect other people enough to look for the logic or belief that differs from yours. Where and why do you diverge? Do you agree on the question and the basic facts? Ask whether establishing a particular fact would change their minds.

Clearly state your own logic. Ask your counterparts to state where they think you are wrong. Let them challenge you. Intelligent people will see that you can listen as well as talk. If you determine there is a basic difference in a belief, agree to disagree.

The Art of Listening

It's my turn to sit back and listen. How can I really hear what someone is trying to say?

It's as easy as crossing the street: Stop, look, and listen. Here are two completely different ways get the most out of listening to someone else:

Listen to what they are saying. Ask questions and really hear the answers. Then ask questions about those answers. Keep digging. If you do not understand, ask for clarification. Restate what you hear to confirm your understanding.

Hear what they are not saying. How many times have you asked a question that was carefully avoided, not fully answered, or hedged? Don't let that happen with you. Read between the lines. Try to understand the speaker's unexpressed self-interest. Be an investigator. Dig. Pretend you're Lieutenant Columbo and keep probing.

How can I get clues to what someone is really thinking?

Study your audience. If your listeners are nodding approval, giving you generous smiles, maintaining eye contact, and expressing lots of ecstatic agreement, you're there. If not, ask them straight out what they are thinking. In situations where direct questions to your listeners are not possible, or are not bringing answers you feel you can trust, look for clues.

People who are feeling positive about what they're hearing or watching often give no signal at all. They may be so entranced or involved in the subject that they simply stare. That's very rarely the case, though, when they're feeling bored, angry, or uncomfortable. So when it comes to looking for signs, you're looking primarily for negative reactions. Watch your audience for these body language clues:

Posture. Leaning too far forward in a chair while listening, with shoulders hunched and slouching, may indicate an opposite conclusion has already been

Ellen's Essentials

At an event to review and evaluate several top execs in a high-profile international conglomerate, I got the chance to watch their CEO speak. Brilliant, handsome, and powerful, either this CEO did not recognize, or chose to ignore, the huge clues the audience gave him that he was completely boring. The audience physically turned away from him and toward each other to whisper their distaste or roll their eyes. Their bodies sagged. People shuffled their feet, played with their food, and tried to escape out the side and back doors. This is a world-class business leader—a big mover and shaker.

Moral of the story: Do not let this happen to you. Watch for the signals. Get coaching. Take a class. Get feedback on your speaking abilities. Get your audience in your court.

If you know people in the embarrassing position of this leader, and have their ear, suggest they work on their performance. Everyone will appreciate you for it.

drawn and that you will be challenged, perhaps competitively. Leaning too far back in a chair while listening may indicate hostility to your ideas, especially when coupled with a hand over the mouth. You may be met with passive aggression.

Arms and hands. Arms folded across the chest, especially while standing, often indicates resistance. Other signs include a hand clapped over the mouth, a finger on the upper lip, or playing with fingers and nails.

Legs and feet. Legs crossed away from you. Knees knocking. Heels or toes tapping. Crossing and uncrossing often. All of these are negative cues.

Eye movement. Lack of eye contact with you, or frequent glances at others, may indicate serious disagreement and disinterest. If combined with a legs apart stance and a knotted brow, you may now anticipate the beginnings of mob action.

Restlessness. Bingo. Restlessness is a *big* clue. Call for a break. Let them stretch.

Mass exodus. Oh boy! Better call me.

What do I do if I don't think my listener is getting my point?

If your listener isn't getting your point—and you don't catch it—you might as well spend the day at the beach. Speaking is not just talking; it is a dialogue. You don't make points by running to your destination and waiting for your listeners to catch up. Speaking is a walk to be taken together. Bring your listeners with you.

If you think you've lost your listeners, stop immediately! Perhaps you loaded on too much detail and not enough of the bottom line. Or perhaps you're not providing enough detail. You won't know unless you ask.

Watch and listen for clues from your audience. Always look for clues. Otherwise, you'll hang yourself.

Ask your listeners to be involved along the way. Ask for feedback as you go. Ask them: "Are you with me?" "Do you agree?" "What are your thoughts on this?" "How do you feel about that?"

Discover their objections and deal with them. "Who has a different opinion?" "What issues do you have with this theory?" "Any objections?"

Get confirmation and agreement that you are all on the same page. "Since I don't hear any objections, I'll take that to mean we're all in agreement on Naomi's proposal. If you agree, nod your heads, and we'll go on."

How can I give my opinion without causing a negative reaction?

Negative reactions are part of life and of business, and it's smart to accept that sometimes negativity happens. Still, it's best not to lob hand grenades. Utilize the following techniques to keep you (and others) from regretting the moment forever.

Consider the time and place. Is this really the best moment for you to voice your opinion? Are other people open to hearing you right now? Generally, it's best to save your criticisms for a private moment.

Be prudent. Did you really hear what you thought you heard? Do you really understand the other point of view? Ask for an explanation or a repetition of the opinion before you react.

Are you ready? Do you have the presence of mind to say it well? There's a win-win way to say everything, but if you don't have it right now, wait.

Be brief and don't argue. Be clear about where your thinking begins, where it goes, and how you get there. Above all, don't try to overpower with repetition.

Be courageous. Speak up. Only when people know what you think can they agree with you.

How can I persuade someone of my point of view?

Give up persuading now. Why waste all that energy?

First, explore what point of view she holds. Uncover exactly why she's sticking to it. Ask a lot of questions and listen carefully to the answers. Be empathetic. After you really understand her position, if you still believe in yours, explain why. State your ideas, facts, and opinions clearly and precisely. If you tend to ramble, focus. Allow her to move off her position and save face.

How do I take a negative audience and persuade them to be on my side?

With honesty, humor, and clarity of thinking. If they don't empathize with you or respect you, they won't listen. If you have a difficult message to deliver, and you want the audience to change their position, you have some work to do. Let's get to it:

Do the research. You need to know what their thinking is. There may be several perspectives out there that oppose your point of view. Know the arguments—and the responses—before you begin to speak.

Respect people. Those you are about to persuade take this issue seriously, too. They see their well-being as tied up in the outcome.

Recognize your responsibility for leadership. By asking for a change of mind, you are proposing to lead. You need to portray a vision of the outcome and tell them why it's in their personal interest or in the broader interest of a community they care about.

Be accessible. Eliminate that big space between you and your audience. Tell a humorous incident about yourself. Be human. Ask for opinions and listen. Smile and remain calm and empathetic to them.

Establish your authority and position. You are representing some viewpoint, company, or interest. Explain your viewpoint authoritatively. Honestly and responsibly represent your organization. Restate the overall goal, and explain why it's in their interest and where the deal is headed. Take questions and give answers.

Be brief. An important element of authority is brevity. No one remembers the 2-hour speech that preceded Lincoln's 2-minute Gettysburg Address.

Accept progress. It's not always necessary to get complete agreement. The fact is, you will not win over everyone, nor will everyone at the meeting have an immediate change of mind. Gaining respect is as important as changing minds.

Thank them and leave. When both viewpoints have been stated, it's time to leave. Don't drag things out beyond their natural ending.

Phone Talk

I'm my own receptionist.
How should I answer the phone?

Ideally, pick up by the second ring. State the name of your company or department, followed by your own name. "Perfect Presentations, Ellen Kaye speaking." On your voice mail message, be brief and speak clearly. Avoid the "uhs" and the long, involved explanations about why you're away from the phone. If you don't answer the phone, and don't forward your calls, it's assumed you're in the bathroom.

I'm about to make a phone call.
How do I get the conversation started?

To prepare good conversation starters and wrap-ups, it is helpful to know the type of person you're calling. If possible, identify beforehand which type of person you are calling: chit-chatters or straight-to-business types. Prepare a strong opener and clear closing specifically for the type of person you're talking to.

If you know you're speaking with a chatter, give that person an invitation to open up by asking generically personal questions: "How about those Braves?" "How's the golf game?" If you're speaking to someone who seems hurried, get right down to business. If in doubt, especially as a junior executive, straight-to-business is often the *safest* choice. Try one of these:

- "Good morning, Jim. I know you are busy so I will get right down to business."

- "Thank you in advance, Mr. Rhodes, for giving me the next ten minutes of your time. Getting down to business . . ."

My phone calls seem to go on forever. How do I wrap it up so I can get on to the next thing?

You have more power if you guide the end of the phone call. Listen for clues in the other person's voice. If your conversation partner sounds distracted, rushed, preoccupied, or needs to end, prepare for the closing. Don't drag out the end of a phone call. Check to see if the other person is ready to close.

If you think it may be appropriate to indicate you want to close, here is how to go about it.

Signal. Indicate that the call is nearing an end.

- "Becky, what would you like to see happen next? I want to make sure I know what you expect before we end this call."

- "I see our time is just about up, Jessie. What else would you like to know?"

- "What others issues do we need to cover in the next four minutes, Sarah, to make this offer complete?"

Summarize. You indicate it's time to close with a summary statement of your understanding of the conversation, what must be done, when, and by whom. "If I understand you correctly, Andrew, I am to do x, y, and z, and call you at 10:30 A.M. next Thursday to share the results with you. At that time you will give me a firm yes or no."

Question. End your summary with a question to confirm this.

- "Morgan, is that your understanding as well?"

- "Alexandra, does that sound fair?"

Define the next step and the time frame. "Tom, thank you so much for your time. I will fax the hard copy of the campaign within the next two hours. I look forward to hearing your feedback."

Confirm with a question. This allows the other person to tell you what will make him happy and end on a positive note.

Don't say anything as definitive as "I'll let you go now!" If the other person had something important to tell you, now you'll never hear it. Too bad, buddy, you just closed the door on yourself. In case the other person was planning to continue on, ask: "Is there anything else you want to cover?" "How are you doing on time?"

End quickly with agreement and consensus. "I like the direction we are going. Thanks again for your time."

Hang up gently. Make sure your phone call is completely disconnected before you say anything else. Don't slam the phone down.

I've got an important phone call this afternoon. How can I prepare for it?

Your phone call always begins long before you pick up your phone. Develop these critical habits for maximizing your preparedness for those very important calls.

1. **E-mail or fax a note to the other person the day before.**

   - Confirm the time you will be calling, the phone number you have for her, and who will call whom.

   - Detail the specifics of the phone meeting.

   - Confirm the agenda.

   - Review your expectations for each person.

   - List your expected outcomes.

Here is how it might all sound when you put these steps together: "I will call you at your East Coast office, at phone number (212) 555-1212, at 4:00 P.M. EST. I look forward to speaking with you about my proposal for the radio ad campaign. Our goals are to introduce you to both campaigns and to get your detailed feedback. If you have any items you wish to address, please e-mail me by this evening so I have time to prepare appropriately for our phone call tomorrow. Thank you very much. I look forward to our phone meeting and this opportunity to work with you on such an important campaign."

2. **Write down the name of the person with whom you are speaking.** Create a Phone Call Goal Checklist and put this item at the top. List the full names and titles of other people or companies who should be discussed. It is astounding how much people forget in the heat of the moment. Even TV anchors have their names written on their teleprompters so they will remember them and remember to say them.

3. **Write down three positive phone habits you want to maintain.** For example: "Speak slowly," "Energy," and "Smile." Tape the paper where you can glance at it throughout your phone call as a reminder.

4. **Write out your agenda and goals.** If you're stuck, think in terms of the who, what, when, where, and why of the deal.

5. **List the key facts to support these goals in order of importance.** List the benefits to your client. Address any objections or concerns you feel may arise. Prepare your resolutions to all of these issues in writing so you will have them ready, in case.

6. **Prepare your physical office space.** Prepare your office space so you can focus on your phone call with a minimum of outside distractions, interruptions, other phone calls, or visitors. Prior to your call, make your space as distraction-free as possible. Go into a *Do Not Disturb* mode.

7. **Set up your tools.** You need all your tools immediately at hand so you can do what you do well. On the left-hand side of your desk, for your continued reference, place the reference notes from Step 2. On the right side of the desk (if you are right-handed), place a note pad and pens to take notes. Take copious notes during a phone call; they are an often underutilized tool. Write down the most important points to refer to in your wrap-up. You also can use the notes to jog your memory after the call is over and to review prior to your next call.

Ellen's
Hot Tips

Controlling a Phone Conversation

Practice. Immediately before beginning the conversation, practice vocalizing or speaking in the tone and volume you plan to use on the phone.

Always use a headset. Keep your hands free to take notes, examine resource documents, grab your water, or throw darts at the photo on your wall.

Be aware. You are unconsciously transmitting your circumstances and feelings to the person on the other end. Be keenly aware of that throughout the conversation.

Lube your voice. Have water readily available, with a straw.

Watch your posture and body language. Stand confidently during the conversation and deliver it as if you were in the same room with the person on the other end of the line. Head up, chest out. Feet parallel, 10 to 12 inches apart, grounded flat on the floor. Don't bend over the keyboard. If you are low and bent over, your body—and your speech—is less powerful.

Always have a spare pen or pencil handy. Of course, it's just when the boss gives you a surprise call and says "Do these eight things immediately and get back to me" that all writing utensils stop working. Don't let yourself get stuck.

Alternatively, have your computer ready to take notes as you speak. Taking notes on paper is quieter and less obtrusive. But if you are a quick typist, entering them on the computer means they can be saved easily as documents and read more easily. The problem with typing is that the computer might be heard. This noise might annoy the person on the other end of the phone, and it might cause him or her to think you're working on something else while you're talking. This is a time when appearing to be multitasking is *not* a plus. Consider saying, "What you say is important and I want to make sure I get all of the details correctly. I will be taking notes on the computer, so you will hear the keys in the background."

How can I feel in control during a phone conversation?

There are several effective strategies for maintaining control during a phone conversation.

1. **Physically get into position.** Start by getting in a position of control to maintain your physical power.

   - Walk around the room to give yourself an energy boost.

   - Keep your body language as powerful as it would be if you were meeting in person eye to eye.

   - Stand up. Remain standing throughout the conversation. If you are sitting, you are too prone to slump, rock back and forth, and engage in other nervous habits. When you are standing you are more focused and more powerful, and this will transmit across the lines.

   - If you have a headset or earpiece, wear it to keep your hands free for gesturing.

2. **Speak on the phone as if you were speaking face to face.** Be fully present.

3. **Use the other person's name often.** Everyone loves to hear the sound of his or her own name.

4. **Manage expectations.** You want a win-win situation, so make sure all concerned are clear on and agree with the expectations and outcomes.

5. **State your objectives.** "I am planning fifteen minutes to review with you how this new ad campaign

will hit your target audience." "It'll take about two minutes to read you the new campaign slogans."

6. **Be concise.** Don't waste your time, or more important, that of your companion.

7. **Speak slowly and clearly.** Listen. Pause.

8. **Don't hog the conversation.** The pig gets fat, but the hog gets slaughtered. You want to be sure you have heard everything the other person wants you to know, so let him or her do most of the talking.

I just got a new speakerphone. Should I use it?

It depends on the situation. Consider your corporate culture. Is this an accepted method of conversation? Do others use this method? What is the purpose of using a speakerphone? How serious or private is the subject matter to be discussed? Consider how people at the other end will feel if you put them on speakerphone.

If your goal is merely a hands-free system, I recommend a headset for convenience, privacy, and a more intimate sound. If you use a speakerphone so you can lean back or keep working, it may result in your caller feeling shouted at. It's certainly not the right way to talk to your boss or a client.

If you decide to use the speakerphone to bring in a third party at your end, you must advise the other party immediately that you are on speakerphone and introduce everyone present. Don't put people in the position where they might inadvertently say something embarrassing, incriminating, or inappropriate.

I'm about to have a conference call. How do I know when to speak?

At the outset of a conference call, the person who set up the call should make introductions, review the agenda and expectations, and explain the rules of the call. For example, "Hello Mr. Cavalier, this is Ellen Kaye in New York. Please say hello to Mr. Gus Hawkins with the XYZ Company from Reno, Nevada, and Ms. Brigette Julien with ABC Company, who is in Paris."

Let them all say their hellos, then take charge again. "To confirm our agenda, the objective of this call is to review the content of my new business etiquette publication and firm up our deadlines. After that I would appreciate your feedback, Mr. Cavalier. Does that work for you?" After he responds, go to the next person. "Mr. Hawkins, I would then appreciate your thoughts. Is that fair?" Await his response. "Ms. Julien will be responsible for foreign rights in Europe and is very familiar with the process. I will ask you to brief us last, Ms. Julien. Is that agreeable?"

I am setting up a conference call. What should I do to get ready for this?

As the leader—the one initiating the conference call—you have the responsibility to expedite communication by sending an e-mail prior to the conference call. Establish the agenda and state the parameters for the call. Explain the format, name the participants, their respective companies, each party's specific role, and whatever other specifics you have. Then everyone will be prepared, and you'll encounter no surprises. As the leader, you have the following responsibilities:

Set and maintain the standards. Some people are experienced and comfortable with this process; others will forget to say their names, may be rude, impatient, interrupt, or be more awkward.

Aid clarity. If all parties are not familiar with each other's voices, remind all parties involved to identify themselves before speaking. "As we don't have the benefit of meeting in person, to make sure we are all clear who is speaking, let's agree to state our names, prior to speaking, each and every time." For example, "This is Ellen Kaye. My feeling about _____." Or, "This is Gus Hawkins. I agree with _____."

Maintain clarity. If someone forgets to state his name, interrupt immediately with, "Forgive the interruption, but it is important we know who is talking so please do remember to introduce yourself." If this continues, a brief, "I apologize, who is speaking?" will suffice.

Moderate. The leader is responsible to moderate the others, particularly when many are vying for the floor. Use the name of the party you plan to have speak. "Let's let Mr. Hawkins have the floor." "Mr. Cavalier, please lead off here." "Ms. Julien, why don't you take this question first."

Make your contribution. If you are not the leader, but a participant in the call, and feel you are not getting the opportunity to speak, ask the leader for help. "Ms. Kaye, I have a point that is pertinent right now. May I share it?"

Be assertive when it's called for. If you are a participant, you may exercise a bit of assertive control and direct the flow of conversation by indicating the next person to speak. For example, "This is Diane Marshall. I believe _____. Now I would like to hear what you have to say on this issue, Ms. Roche." Or, "Please share your thoughts on this, Mr. Nader, before we hear from Mr. Block."

I have to leave a greeting on my voice mail. What should it sound like?

Professional, crisp, and clear. No long or awkward pauses, no giggling, no weird background noises, music, or distracting sounds. Keep it short, sweet, and to the point. People are too busy to listen to meandering explanations of why you're not answering your phone.

Ellen's Essentials

When leaving a phone message, it is rude to neglect to leave your phone number. Even if you think they have it, it is thoughtless to expect another person to go hunting for a phone number. Make it easy for someone to return your call. If you want a call back, always leave your area code and phone number. Say the number, once slowly, and repeat it. Any smart businessperson will do this automatically. Be sure you're one of them.

It's usually the harried receptionist who takes it as a personal affront when asked to repeat a number. Even then, be conscious that he or she is the gatekeeper so be courteous enough to say, "Please repeat that number for me, just to be sure I said it correctly."

You've reached Phyllis Manrod, executive assistant to Ellen Kaye, president of Perfect Presentation. Your call is important so please leave your name and number, whether you think we have it or not, and a brief (or detailed) message. I will get back to you within twenty-four hours. Thank you.

Technology being what it is, answering machines automatically give the time and date of the message. If yours doesn't, buy a new one.

When leaving an important voice mail message, I freeze up, stutter, or blab on and on. I hang up and hate myself for being totally unprofessional. What can I do?

The following advice will make leaving voice mail messages a piece of cake. Take it easy on yourself and check things off as you prepare.

Make notes before you pick up the phone. Outline the main points you want to make. Write out your script word for word. Practice it several times. Stick to it exactly. Then dial and go for it with gusto.

Speak slowly and clearly; leave your first and last name, then spell your last name. Slowly. "Hello David. This is Ellen Kaye from Perfect Presentation.

That's Ellen, E-l-l-e-n, Kaye, K-a-y-e, from Perfect Presentation in Scottsdale, Arizona."

Leave your number slowly if you want a call back. Too many people neglect to do this at all, but almost as bad are people who leave their number but say it so quickly that even with repeated playbacks it is still unintelligible. Leave your phone number and say it twice, slowly. Even if you know they have it, someone else may be jotting the message down, or they may be traveling or not have their PDA. Who knows? Who cares? The only important issue is you want them to call you back. So, *leave your number.*

Avoid playing phone tag. Leaving more than a "Please call me," or "I am responding to your call," is up to you. I personally prefer it when people leave a very detailed message. I want to know the subject of the call so I can respond with real information. Phone tag, an annoying waste of everyone's time, is then minimized.

"This will be the only call I am going to make." The first time I heard this I thought it quite rude. Now I appreciate it. It tells me clearly and in no un-certain terms that the ball is in my court. If commu-nication is to happen, it's my turn to initiate it. If you use this, try to remember to say, "Thank you" after-ward to soften the impact.

Keep your voice well modulated, pleasant, and professional. This sounds simple, but in rushed, high pressure, often infuriating or disappointing business situations, this can be very hard to do.

Never leave a voice message when you are angry or upset. Force yourself to wait, no matter how long. In fact, never do anything when you are angry or upset.

Say "Thank you" at the end of a call. Even if you did the work and you deserve the thanks, it's a nice habit and shows your thoughtfulness. There is another use of the final "Thank you." A well-placed thank-you can be intimidating when both parties know the recipient did not deserve it.

Potpourri

Small talk is such a waste of time, and I resent having to do it at work, but apparently it is now part of my job. How do I get over my dislike of small talk?

You can't. Not as long as your perception of "small talk" is "meaningless, demeaning, wasteful chatter." The implied meaning is "I am wasting my time and talents." Never underestimate the power of small talk or the art of

The Perfect Presentation of "Bonding Conversation"

Never make small talk again! Here's how.

Change the paradigm. Start thinking of all your conversations within the context of important, meaningful, profitable "bonding conversation."

Bonding conversation is not boring, and don't you be either. Honor yourself, your time, and your energy. Be prepared to utilize this time well.

Bonding conversation is an opportunity to get a feel for a new person and begin a new relationship, whether with a potential client or a new friend.

Bonding conversation can be delicate, nuanced, and entirely enjoyable. Bonding conversation is the cup of coffee, the cocktails, or the milk and cookies shared between people.

The real meaning lies not in the discussion of the weather or the care and feeding of a pet. The meaning and purpose of bonding conversation is to get a sense of the other person and to learn about that person's values, thoughts, and perspectives.

Talk about things that matter to you. Mention something you just learned or read. Bring up a weird factoid, an amazing or amusing statistic. Start a dialogue.

Ask questions and listen to the answers. Ask questions from the information you learned in the answers to previous questions. Be curious but do not pry.

Once you change your paradigm and start to use these tips and techniques, the benefits to you are endless. You will develop more friends, cultivate more clients, and enjoy your life more. As you open the door to more conversations, you will experience more bonding and more success.

conversation. Conversations—even the cautious opening gambits we call "small talk"—are the building blocks of long-term business and personal relationships.

How can I say "No"?

No is a difficult word to say for both men and women. Furthermore, unpleasant as the idea is, each sex says it differently.

Is your plate too full, or do you simply not want to do the request at hand? Should be no problem to say no, right? Wrong. Guilt makes it very hard for most of us to say no. Mother probably told you "A busy person gets things done." Sometimes, other concerns come into play. You may have self-worth issues. Perhaps you beat yourself up when you don't say yes. Is it the "shoulda, coulda, woulda" syndrome?

Whatever your particular issues, here is a script to help you get to a simple "no." It can be difficult, so let's practice together.

- Say it with me now: "No." Too tough? OK. OK. Let's rethink this. Hmmm. Try this. This is way better. Say, "No. Thank you."

- Only if saying something more is *absolutely required* should you even think of adding anything. If something is absolutely required, try "I am very flattered/honored/grateful/delighted to be asked. However, I must say no."

- Or, if it is a time issue, try this to soften the blow. "No. Thank you. Not at this time anyway." Resist the temptation to add: "Possibly next week/month/year."

- When saying no, you may win favor by suggesting someone else whom you feel may be up to the task.

A friend? An enemy? In fact, you may be doing both parties a favor. Or, you may end up with one or both of them hating your guts. Beware.

- Try to avoid snippy remarks ("I would love to do that. When hell freezes over.") no matter how much fun. Above all, always be polite.

Really, the only way to refuse is the way Nancy Reagan said it: "Just say No." That way you've got no regrets, no explanations, no guilt, no excuses, no worries, and no "I'll think about it."

I forgot someone's name and I'm about to introduce this individual to someone else. How can I cover?

As discreetly as possible, quietly ask for the person's name again. A quick, "I'm sorry, I want to introduce you to Mr. Roberts and I want to get your name exactly right. Would you repeat it for me, please?" should suffice.

A helpful memory technique is to repeat the other person's name three times in conversation shortly after being introduced. This trick carves their name indelibly in your brain. Even if it doesn't, it will certainly endear you to those people.

Many people have this problem, so you needn't be overly concerned. The worst that happens is that you'll have to confess your forgetfulness and ask again.

How can I be the person who controls the conversation?

Here's a really bad idea: Shout. Speak louder than the person with whom you are fighting for control. If he raises his voice, follow suit. Don't even think about who is listening or whom you may be disturbing.

To be in control means to understand what the conversation needs to accomplish. A business conversation should have a beginning, middle, and end. Organize a logical sequence of points to be made to get your conclusion. Make notes. Important conversations should be planned and rehearsed.

Ellen's Hot Tips

Delivering Information and Controlling the Floor

Plan and rehearse your approach and desired delivery. Then ask a colleague or friend to be your antagonist. As such, that person must alternately play the courteous listener and the aggressive, know-it-all, rude interrupter, constantly challenging your delivery. Work it until you are comfortable. Then the real delivery will be a breeze.

In a perfect world, your audience may allow you to give your presentation without interruption, recognizing they get your best that way. More often, however, your listeners will interrupt you with questions, changing your presentation substantially.

To regain control, ask your questioners what their most important concerns are. Reorganize your delivery to answer those points first and then get back on track.

I've been asked a question, and I don't know the answer. How can I avoid looking dumb?

There are several good ways to deal with not knowing the answer to a question.

Buy time. Restate the question. This gives you that extra moment to pull your thoughts together and come up with an answer.

Ask a question about the sense of the question. Ask your questioner to rephrase.

Don't answer a question you can't answer well. An ill-conceived answer is worse than no answer.

If you don't know, admit it. Then set a time and date by which you *will* have the answer. "Good question, Susan. I am afraid I don't have all the facts on that issue for you right now. Please give me a call tomorrow at around noon and I will have it for you."

Delegate the question. If someone is present who you think will have the information, pass the question to him. Jim, my colleague, may have the answer you're looking for."

Suggest another person or resource that might have the answer. "Our international division will have the exact figures on that. Please give Mr. Gaugnaut a call."

I just received a compliment. How do I respond?

Now this is really simple. Look the person directly in the eyes, smile, and—watch my lips—say, "Thank you." Anything less ("Oh, this old thing? I've had it forever.") disparages the person who complimented you.

Someone just offended me. Do I say anything?

First, consider the source. Was it someone whose support you need? Was it someone everyone knows is out on a limb already? Was it public or private?

If it was someone whose support you need, be direct and ask the reason. Say you didn't understand the comment and need to know what you're missing. Allow the person to apologize, even if it's lame. Save your ruthless cruelty for a real war; preserve an ally. If it was Tom the Office Fool, everyone understands. You'll all torture him later.

It's normally best to simply ignore insults and offenses, but there are times when a public insult needs an intelligent public response. If you do decide to respond to a significant personal insult, think it through, and choose your time and place. Respond with dignity.

I want to join a group of people who are talking to each other. Can I join them without interrupting?

If you're considering edging your way into a circle of people, stop and think. Then think again. You may want to join them, but will they want you? If you have any doubt, don't. If you decide to join in, walk up and enter the physical space of the others. Watch carefully for their body language and listen carefully for their verbal cues.

> *Observe before you interrupt and your presence will never be considered an interruption.*
>
> *—Ellen A. Kaye*

If welcomed, you're in, and you made the right decision. Listen quietly until you catch up with the conversation or are directly addressed, before you speak up.

Ellen's Essentials

A distressed client recently blew it when she saw two of her biggest clients, with whom she had become friends, talking to each other. In her excitement, she walked up and with a great big smile said, "How great to find the two of you here together. I wanted to see you both today." Unfortunately, she was so preoccupied with herself that she totally neglected to observe their emotional states and physical cues before she barged in. She interrupted their very serious, very private, very emotional conversation.

Don't do this to yourself or others. It can be painful and embarrassing.

If you see people turning away from you, refusing eye contact, or lowering their voices, take the clue. You're not welcome. Promptly excuse yourself. "I can see you are talking something through. Hope to see you later. Please excuse me."

DIFFICULT SITUATIONS

- How to Handle Difficult Clients
- Mistakes Happen
- Body Politics
- Teamwork Troubles
- Potpourri

WHEN YOU ARE MOVING THROUGH YOUR DAYS and all is well, one success after another seems to fall in your lap. But then, out of the blue, disaster strikes. Instead of crying, "Why me?" learn how to handle those difficult and trying moments. You're not a deer caught in the headlights; you're a thinking, rational human being. Try to remember that. Also, it doesn't hurt a bit to have worked out some strategies in advance for dealing with unscripted surprises that have the potential to send your career crashing on the rocks or soaring to the skies. This chapter is full of unexpected moments and suggestions for taking advantage of them. Use these turning-point moments to set your feet right back on the fast track to success.

How to Handle Difficult Clients

I have to work with the client everyone loves to hate. How can I work with this difficult person?

Welcome the opportunity. Working with this client carefully and diligently, with goodwill and humor, will demonstrate to your boss and colleagues that you are a team player with a good attitude. The fact that there will be setbacks is predictable, which will ease the pressure on you somewhat. Here are ideas to help you handle this difficult situation.

Between you and the difficult client. Determine what makes this client so difficult. If the client is asking for greater effort, take on the challenge with goodwill. If your work or your results are never good enough, do a reality check. If your client truly does not follow the material, convert to an "ends justify the means" approach. It is important to move on to action; suggest that your solution be adopted on a limited basis.

Between you and your boss. As you attempt to meet and surpass the extreme requirements of a demanding client, communicate with your boss. In situations like this, you cannot allow differing expectations to exist. Let your boss know about your successes and failures. Ask for advice!

Verify with your boss that your effort will be profitable to the company, now or in the future. In some cases, high demands by clients mean working at a loss for the future carrot. Let your boss determine whether there really is a carrot and its worth. Ask your boss why this client is still using your company. Perhaps your group has indeed met the requirements and the client merely keeps raising the bar. Is the client methodically keeping you off balance?

Don't say things are going well if they are not. Your boss must know the issues and be prepared to deal with them.

My client stands too close when he talks to me. What should I do?

Every living being has unique personal space boundaries. We are territorial, and when someone or something gets

Ellen's Hot Tips

Observing and Exploring Personal Space Boundaries

Observe people as they stand and talk to each other. It's fascinating to watch as the person with the smaller personal space boundary—let's call her Ms. Iwanta Getclose—unconsciously and repeatedly invades the personal space of Mr. Asfaraway Aspozibull. He subconsciously needs much more personal space. Even during a brief and friendly conversation, she may literally back him into a corner.

If Mr. Asfaraway Aspozibull can subtly move himself back, away from the offending party, he's lucky for the moment. However, this will be a consistent problem between certain people if their personal space boundaries are very different.

If uncomfortable, you may want to mention this in a gentle way. Put the onus on yourself. "Gee Ms. Getclose, I need a little bit more elbow room here. I am going to back up a little." Alternatively, "I'm sorry, but I am a little claustrophobic and need some more space. Would you mind scooting over a bit?"

too close, we feel threatened and uncomfortable. We respond by fight or flight. (This is also why it is unwise to get too close to a strange dog or to go into the iguana cage at the zoo—especially without your shoes on.)

If this is a sexual harassment issue, act immediately. If it feels wrong, it is wrong. Move away immediately, with or without explanation. Men, be sensitive to this. The woman you are standing next to often does not want to be as close to you as you do to her. If you see her backing away from you, stop crowding her. It will do wonders for your reputation in the long run.

Sit down. If this is not a sexual harassment issue or you do not want to address the proximity issue at the moment, one temporary remedy is to suggest you both be seated. The office, lounge, or conference room furniture will then dictate the intimacy. In a pinch, you can suggest you have a cold and ask for distance. However, you must realize this is the chicken's way out and the problem will surely come up again.

I just noticed our biggest client is about to go on stage to accept an award and his fly is open. Do I do or say anything?

If you want to be a hero, absolutely. Gently touch his arm, lean into him so no one else will hear you, and simply say, "Michael, your fly is open." If you are too far away, signal his attention, then indicate with a discreet gesture so he will get the message and save himself embarrassment.

Mistakes Happen

My proposal was shot down in front of everyone. How can I stay composed?

The measure of a person is how he or she accepts and deals with the rough times, not the easy ones. Setbacks of this nature are part of the territory in business life. There will be additional opportunities for success as well as for being shot down.

Interestingly, a failure can contribute as much to your next achievement as a success. Rather than adopting an "all or nothing" attitude, be prepared to learn from experience either way.

Remaining composed serves the vital purpose of allowing you to gauge the reasons for this setback. Did your idea have flaws others brought up? Incorporate those ideas in your next proposal, and perhaps get more prior feedback next time. Did you fail to anticipate an objection, or were you unprepared for certain questions? Did you give a poor presentation of a good idea?

Don't struggle or plead. At a certain point, you will know whether you can save yourself. Thank your critics for their input. For your own purposes, privately review the things you have learned. You might offer to meet the objections of the group, and propose again, if no final decision will be made immediately.

If no second chance exists, be prepared to describe to your boss or others exactly why the proposal did not satisfy the needs of your critics.

I just stuck my foot in my mouth. How do I regroup?

To extricate your foot from your mouth, a major apology is generally required. Leaving the room with the insult or faux pas hanging in the air makes the situation permanent. The thing about making a fool of yourself is that it happens without warning. Say so. Self-deprecating humor is a possible way out with some people, but with others you will need to spend some time in silent embarrassment. Apologize and move on.

I think I just offended somebody. What should I say?

Ask if what you said was offensive. "When I said _____, I noticed your reaction. Was what I said offensive to you? If it was, I apologize."

I just lost my temper. How can I regroup?

Consider how you feel when people lose their temper with you. Not too pleasant, is it? Try to remember what's really important. Losing your temper is often the result of being overly concerned about something, at least momentarily. To recover, do the following in order:

- Pull yourself together. Let someone else take the lead. Drink a glass of water.

- Apologize immediately, clearly, and simply.

- Don't try to defend yourself.

- Move on smoothly by changing the subject, asking someone else to take over, or excusing yourself, if possible.

- Cry on a shoulder, complain relentlessly, and take the blame.

Body Politics

My colleague is touchy-feely, and I'm feeling uncomfortable. What should I do?

Ideally, colleagues can be told directly when personal space invasion is unwelcome. In general, the workplace is

Ellen's Essentials

Each culture defines personal space boundaries differently. Make it a habit to observe and honor unique practices other than your own. Your knowledge of cultural values and customs can make or break a big deal.

not a place for contact of this sort. You will benefit your colleague by making it clear that your professional standards require more personal space and distance and that anything less will compromise your effectiveness. Be matter of fact. No one can challenge you on this. If you want to send a clear message that closeness is unwelcome outside the workplace as well, say so. A person taking small liberties will often increase them if no negative response is given.

If you don't feel comfortable telling your colleague directly, or if this may be a sexual harassment issue, respond immediately. Go to your mentor, your boss, or the HR department and ask for their professional aid. Your HR department in particular will know just how to handle this situation. They undoubtedly have procedures to address this type of problem.

How can I stay focused when I am tired?

If you are having trouble paying attention due to fatigue, here are several suggestions for both external and internal stimulants.

External Stimulants

- Coffee, chocolate, caffeine in any format.

- Stay busy. Take notes.

- Take copious notes and write them in a foreign language. As you force yourself to concentrate, you will stay focused.

- Give yourself pain that is constant and excruciating.

- If you are working with others, go out for a beer.

- Join the conversation. Participate and ask questions so the adrenaline will kick in. Be more active, not less. It's a little like slapping your own cheek.

Internal Stimulants

- Realize your job depends on it. When working toward a deadline and you are tired, establish small milestones such as time deadlines for your work. How much do you need done in the next few hours? If the overall schedule can work, then allow yourself a few moments' rest at each milestone.

- Do the organizational work (not just the content) up front. When you are organized for the presentation, if time runs out for preparation, you can still present, even if you end up a bit short on content. Changes will doubtless be requested, and missing material can be inserted later.

I'm starving at a cocktail party. How can I find food?

Be a detective. Ask the servers! Having come from the kitchen, they will know what's in the kitchen or know where to find food. It's no sin to admit to your group that your busy schedule prevented your last meal and you must eat now to remain upright. Perhaps the server can have something small prepared for you, or perhaps you can visit the kitchen. In general, if you want to eat, stand near the entrance, where the servers are entering from the kitchen with the hors d'oeuvres.

I burped. Loudly. Now what do I do?

Do not make a big deal out of this. In a quiet and humble voice, only loud enough for those who had the misfortune of hearing you burp, simply say, "Excuse me."

What do I do if I have something in my teeth?

> *You sound like a really attractive guy!*
>
> —*Gilda Radner as Roseanna Roseannadanna*

Get it out as soon as possible. Excuse yourself from the table, go to the restroom, and clean up. Toward that end, I always recommend carrying some kind of floss, toothpick, or, best yet, a small travel toothbrush and toothpaste.

When I get really nervous, I get cotton mouth, I sweat, and my stomach makes noises. Help!

Forget getting down to business and don't even think of fast tracking. Get a job in the mailroom. Alternatively, try the following:

For cotton mouth sufferers. I recommend you be sure to always carry your own concoction of nonsparkling (no gas in the water or you), room temperature (so as not to freeze or chill your vocal cords) pure water with a dash of fresh lemon (to cut the phlegm and prevent cotton mouth). Be sure to filter out the lemon pits.

For sweating. There is one antiperspirant of nuclear strength. Ask your pharmacist. If you are further concerned, try using under-arm shields. They attach to your blouse or shirt and will prevent moisture from showing. They can be tricky, so be sure to sew or pin them on your garment correctly or they'll do no good.

For stomach noises. Try the over-the-counter remedies to prevent your stomach from going acidic, which is what usually provokes the growling. If you are using a lavaliere microphone, keep it as far away from your noisy stomach as possible, for everyone's sake. If your stomach is a serious problem, see a doctor immediately.

Teamwork Troubles

My rival just took a cheap shot at me. How should I respond?

If you are blessed with ready wit, use your humor to respond. Be gracious and make the comment irrelevant. Revenge is less acceptable than the unskillful comment that prompted it. You may or may not choose to expose what a cheap shot it was, depending on the specifics of the situation (who else is present, the power and political prestige of your rival). If the comment was damaging, follow up privately with your boss. Reestablish your competence. Remember, most bosses don't want to manage infighting.

My coworker is interrupting me. What should I do?

You could object. But the better course is to ask yourself what the interruptions stem from. There are three potential reasons people interrupt. Are you being interrupted because your coworker suffers from one of them? If so, here is how to deal with the situation.

Poor social skills. Gently point out how you feel when you are interrupted. "You seem to interrupt me a lot. I want to let you know how I feel when that happens. I feel angry/anxious/unappreciated/unheard/disrespected. I would really appreciate it if you would try to let me finish before you begin. Does that sound fair?"

Unsophisticated competition. Make a deal. "Let's both try not to interrupt each other. I feel it would be more constructive if we let each other finish our thoughts before speaking. Does that work for you?"

The "know it all" syndrome. Establish the agenda in advance so that the interruption, by definition, is an interruption and not part of the flow of a back-and-forth discussion. To avoid constant interruptions, state what you intend to say: "I want to give you my conclusion on this point, and the reasons I believe in it." This will raise the ante in terms of the rudeness quotient of interrupting. If necessary, prepare and distribute a written summary for all to follow.

Here is another possibility you'll need to consider: Perhaps you're being interrupted because you're not communicating efficiently. If your explanations get repetitive or veer off topic, take a hint from the interruption and cut it short.

My coworker says one thing but doesn't seem entirely sincere. How can I read my colleague's real meaning?

Get together with your coworker and discuss your concerns. You may find that your coworker agrees in principle but has unvoiced objections. Your coworker may be relieved to express what was being held back and appreciate the opportunity and your interest in clearing the air. The worst-case scenario—your coworker may have another agenda.

Here are some solid suggestions to start you thinking about how to approach your coworker with your concerns.

Set the stage. When and where you address this issue is important. *When:* Choose your moment carefully. Choose a time when you feel your coworker will be most relaxed and open. You may want to invite your coworker to lunch, or coffee, or to take a walk in the park. *Where:* Chose a private safe space within which you feel you will both be able to talk freely, away from the everyday office distractions and prying eyes and ears.

Set your goals and the agenda. Your goal is to create a win-win situation for all involved: you, your coworker, the company, and the client. Assess your individual views to make sure you are on the same page.

Establish the emotional tone. Share that you have some concerns. Make it your problem, not your colleague's. For the good of the project, your boss, the client, and everyone's careers, explain that you feel clear and honest communication is vital. Suggest that you both may simply have different ways of communicating and this is an attempt on your part to get on the same page. Share that you appreciate her time and effort to clear up your confusion and cooperate. Point out that letting things slide, harboring lingering doubts, lack of trust or resolution, helps no one. Additionally, when people agree to the same conclusion for completely different reasons, it is a recipe for failure. The next decision may bring unexpected disagreement due to the hidden differences.

Get to the meat of the matter. Review your thoughts and opinions on the issues first to set a tone of honesty and forthrightness. Then ask your coworker to do the same. Perhaps your coworker will now be forthcoming.

You may assume deviousness when, in fact, it may not be there. Use your intuition. Trust your gut. Interrogate the heck out of your colleague—politely, in a good way.

Ultimately—depending on the variable personalities, the company's culture, and the politics involved—you may need to go to your boss.

My coworker smells bad. Should I say something?

If it's an unusual circumstance, and you're not close, no. Let it pass. But if it's a daily occurrence, then yes. The question, of course, is what, when, and how. This is a touchy personal situation that must be dealt with discreetly, diplomatically, and in private. If you feel you cannot do this, you have two other choices: Either leave your coworker a copy of this book with a tab on the personal hygiene pages or ask the boss handle it.

Potpourri

The elevator door is opening and I'm about to get in. Where do I look? Where do I stand?

It is always amazing to me how frequently people waiting for an elevator do not move aside so the people inside may get out first. Use your common sense and understand the following points of etiquette:

Waiting Outside an Elevator to Get On

- Move aside so there is adequate space for those who need to get off to do so.

- While waiting, politely hold open the closing doors for others to exit.

Entering an Elevator

- Enter the elevator briskly.

- Immediately move to the back wall, then turn around to face the doors.

- Enter and move to one side, press the Door Open button.

- Keep your arms close at your sides.

- If carrying parcels and packages, keep them tight to your body to allow space for others.

- Keep your handbag and other items in front of you and within sight. This is a great place for pickpockets.

If You Cannot Reach the Elevator Buttons

- In a polite but clearly audible voice, say "Would you please press seven for me? Thank you."

- If the elevator is crowded and in a busy city where everyone is used to the protocol, simply say "Seven, please," pause to give someone time to do this, then say, "Thanks."

Exiting an Elevator

- You have the right of way.

- Exit quickly so those behind you may exit also and those waiting outside may enter after you have exited.

- If you need to exit and are in the rear of the elevator, say "Out, please" as you approach your floor. This will give the people in front of you a heads-up that you will be needing to exit. They will move aside or even step off the elevator to allow for your exit.

- Obviously, if you are in the front of a crowded elevator and hear "This is my stop," you should be courteous and immediately move to the nearest side to let that party exit.

How can I act interested even when I'm not?

It's your *job* to be interested. Showing boredom or disinterest will surely cost you a client, perhaps a good review, even your employment. Your client's and your boss's business needs and personal interests are all part of the world in which you have chosen to seek success. Demonstrate your interest by asking questions. People like to talk about themselves. Develop the skills and habits of asking questions about their activities and interests. Probe for information.

Feign physical attentiveness. Lean forward. Nod your head at the appropriate times. Fake it until you make it.

Oh, no. My zipper is down. What should I do?

Quickly and discreetly turn away from the hoards of amazed, horrified, stunned, gawking onlookers, and zip it immediately. To avoid this embarrassing moment, after zipping up your pants, always push the zipper flap flat to lock it in place.

My desk is so cluttered, people look at it with horror. How can I change my ways?

You've heard people claim a cluttered desk is the sign of an intelligent mind. With all due respect, I must disagree. Consider the unprofessional impression this makes. Right or wrong, we all make split-second judgments about others. People assume you handle your professional business dealings, contracts, and responsibilities the same way you handle your desk. A desk is a business tool. Keep it clean, clear, and uncluttered. For more on how to get your workspace into tip-top shape, consult the following checklist on organizing your office.

Ellen's Believe It or Not

A bright and talented client in New York City who wants to be on the fast track was inadvertently holding herself back by refusing to acknowledge the unprofessionalism of a messy, disorganized desk and office. In addition, her appearance was dated and unprofessional, as she was still clinging to her "college look" ten years laer. Her boss and her boss's boss retained me to help her look more professional and be more efficient.

Don't let your ego, self-righteousness, stubbornness, or a friend stand in your way. Get down to business and spend a few hours after work getting organized. The first time through takes the most time. After that, it's just a matter of maintenance.

Ellen's
Checklist

Organizing and Maintaining a Professional Office

1. If you have to look for anything, you're disorganized. Step back and evaluate your workspace. If it looks disorganized, it probably is.

(continues)

(continued)

2. **Keep everything in the same place, all the time.** If you know where everything is, you will not waste time or energy searching.

3. **Organize your office.** Sort out desk, drawers, and closets with the items you use most often in the most accessible places.

4. **Keep like things together.** Staplers with the staples and the staple remover. Scotch tape, masking tape, and packing tape together. Sort books by topic so, when you need something, you can find it easily and quickly.

5. **Color-code your files.** The colors don't matter as along as you stay consistent. Red for urgent. Green for clients. Blue for basics. White for general information. Pink for personal. Orange for projects. It's your business; you figure it out.

6. **Read a few good books on organization.** You will benefit from their suggestions for the rest of your life.

7. **If you know people who are very efficient, ask them how they do it.** Admit you are looking for ideas. Seek out special tips or tricks for getting and staying organized.

8. To start, take a weekend, weeknight, or early morning. Clear everything off all the counters and empty the drawers. Ask yourself: Do I absolutely need this? How often do I use this? Would I really miss this if I threw it out? Try to get rid of as much as possible. Whatever you keep, put it into its permanent place.

Chapter 4

MEETINGS

- Set Yourself Up for Success
- Whose Body Is This Anyway?
- Meet Your Boss on Your Terms
- Potpourri

WHEN NOTICE OF A MEETING CIRCULATES through the office, you can almost hear the air leave the building. Nobody on the fast track to success wants to spend valuable time in yet another meeting. How can you be leaping tall buildings in a single bound when you're stuck in a meeting until your eyes glaze over? This chapter provides lots of ways to turn an otherwise mundane meeting into a gift for you—another chance to sell yourself to your clients, your coworkers, and your boss. Polish up your expectations, put a spring in your step and a sparkle in your eye, and get on with *your* program. Here's how.

Set Yourself Up for Success

How do I get organized for meetings?

To minimize personal distractions during a meeting, I have created a chart for meeting planning. Take a few minutes

Ellen's Checklist

Meeting Planning Chart

Day and Date _____

Clients _____

Participants _____

Location _____

Purpose _____

My Agenda _____

To Do _____

Send _____

Get _____

New Ideas _____

Miscellaneous _____

_____

_____

before the meeting to fill out this checklist and you will be able to focus on the meeting once it begins.

I have to give a report in a meeting. What's the most powerful way to present the information?

This is the time for the tried and true.

- Tell them what you are going to tell them.

- Tell them.

- Tell them what you told them.

When giving a report, it is important to think like a teacher. The knowledge you have is not a secret to be guarded until the end of your presentation. At the beginning, state your conclusions. Then discuss and show the detail. In the end, summarize again.

Think carefully about your material. What are the significant points? What is the clearest explanation? The power of the report lies in what the participants take away. Don't try to teach the full inventory of detailed knowledge you have assembled. Clearly state your conclusions and provide an explanation of how your information affects your audience.

I have written a report for an upcoming meeting. What else should I do to get ready for this meeting?

In giving a report, all the issues of personal appearance, body language, and voice projection are critical (see chapter 5 for a discussion of many of these issues). These personal issues are central to your success in these milestone moments as well as throughout your career.

Rehearse your delivery in a sequence that includes all the information and leads to your conclusion. Always prepare an outline—even if you don't think you will need it. Always take it with you when presenting. Perhaps your rehearsal and visual memory of the outline will be sufficient to give you confidence for a presentation from memory. However, when you get nervous, you never know when your memory will go.

Decide what media are most appropriate for your report. Will you distribute color copies of outlines and charts? Will you give a presentation from a laptop with a projector? Will the room have sophisticated technology? Get staff help to demonstrate the equipment and their assurance that they will be on call prior to your meeting. Test the equipment a few hours before the meeting.

I'm heading into a "see and be seen" meeting. I want to attract maximum attention. What should I do?

Make yourself immediately noticeable. Wait until most people are seated before you enter. Enter in the front of the room. Look out at the other attendees. Wave, smile, and say hello to people. Establish yourself as a high-status person with presence and confidence.

Make a point of greeting the superior person(s) in the room, either aloud or with a confident smile and nod. Indicate you have seen or met him before to show you have a past relationship with him. "Good to see you again, Mr. Mayor." Don't slink in or stumble over people. Act as though you not only belong at the meeting but will be an important contributor. Looking cool is its own reward.

Physical appearance counts. Posture should be perfect. Stand up straight, shoulders back, chin up. Balance your weight on both feet equally. No slouching or standing on one foot.

Arrange to have a covert ally at the meeting. You sit at one end of the table; your ally sits at the other. When you speak, speak directly to him in a loud voice. "Alex, I have an idea you may want to use!" You are speaking to the end of the table, and your ally is nodding and responding positively. The other members are caught in the middle, making them more likely to jump on your bandwagon and respond positively as well.

I'm meeting with my boss's boss in two days. How can I prepare?

Congratulations! Face time with the boss's boss is an exciting opportunity for getting down to business and fast tracking your career. Be ready to talk about your work and yourself. Here's what to do:

Write out the status of each assignment on your plate. Summarize what you have accomplished in each project or account over the last 6 months. Organize a brief summary so you can answer with ease and without excessive detail. Be prepared with good language. Take some time to choose key words and phrases that will put your accomplishments in a positive light.

Identify steps you can take to put each item in a better position. You may be lacking a simple step to complete a project. Get answers on open items and take steps before the meeting to build your accomplishments to their best possible position in the time you have.

Before you're asked about you, make sure you know you. What are your aspirations? How do you view your work? What gives you the greatest sense of accomplishment? What have you learned about your industry? What do you want to know more about? What philosophy guides you? Are you ready for more? Demonstrate that you have thoughts about your career. In a large company, your boss will have similar thoughts about moving up.

Be ready to accept a task, suggestion, or department goal. Show initiative and enthusiasm.

Plan to be early. Skip going out the night before. This is not the day to make anyone wait.

Prepare your clothes in advance. Make sure you have what you need and be sure your clothing is in excellent condition to prevent surprises.

Make the meeting time count. Meetings like this are usually brief—20 or 30 minutes. Your good preparation will make the meeting sizzle!

Whose Body Is This Anyway?

My meeting is right after lunch. What should I eat for lunch?

Take an early lunch or eat lightly to avoid the drowsiness that comes from a bigger meal. Don't undermine your performance by requiring your body to digest while you need to be sharp. At midmorning, a carbohydrate-rich meal will give you time to store energy and feel very comfortable at meeting time.

As it gets closer to meeting time, if you haven't eaten, avoid rich, heavy foods, which may give you stomach cramps, gas, bloating, and other unmentionables when

How to Avoid a Dietary Disaster

The real question is what *shouldn't* you eat for lunch? If you have a meeting coming up right after lunch, just say no to these food and drink choices:

Dairy foods. Dairy can cause phlegm, which leads to annoying throat clearing and coughing.

Carbonated water and beverages. Burping will not be the best message for you to send.

Very hot drinks. Don't burn or numb your tongue or the roof of your mouth if you will be speaking.

Very cold drinks and food. They cause your throat to constrict and make it difficult to speak.

mixed with tension. Eat slowly. Limit yourself to light foods and just a small meal. Remember to protect your clothes and leave time to freshen up (brush your teeth and use a mouthwash) and check your appearance (reapply lipstick, tuck in your shirt or blouse to keep it in place, dust your shoulders for dandruff or stray hairs, straighten your tie, and give yourself a pep talk).

Icy drinks. They can leave you cold and shaking.

Ice cream or a milkshake. The worst. Dairy and cold.

Spicy foods. Spare yourself the indigestion; spare your neighbor the gas.

Tuna with onions. Bad breath.

Heavy foods, carbohydrates, and turkey. These foods will make you drowsy.

Salty foods. These will dry out your mouth.

Caffeine. If you're not used to it, it can make you very jittery.

Alcohol. Self-explanatory.

How do I sit at a meeting?

Always sit, stand, and look polished and professional. Here's how:

- Lower yourself gently into the chair. Don't plop or drop into a chair, nonverbally declaring your exhaustion or your weight. That's more than anyone wants to know.

- Once on the chair, push your posterior to the back of the chair.

Ellen's Hot Tips

The Art of Sitting

The following positions are totally inappropriate in the office if you are getting down to business and want to fast track your career.

- Don't even think about leaning back in your chair so the front two legs are off the ground.
- No rapid, or even slow, swiveling.
- No putting your arms behind your head.
- Don't slouch, and certainly don't rest your head on your hand.

- Your legs and feet should be placed directly in front of you. Be sure to move your feet all the way in front of you. Don't leave them on either side of your chair as if you are ready to bolt.

- No jiggling your high heels off your toes, ladies.

- Men, in particular, no bouncing your legs or shaking your foot or knees. This is extremely bad manners and a huge red flag indicating your nervousness.

- Ladies, and we mean this in the best way, keep those knees together when wearing a skirt.

- Men, please do the same on that much anticipated and revitalizing "wear-a-kilt-to-work" day.

- Once sitting at the meeting, arrange your reading, writing, and report materials neatly. Forearms on the table are okay if you'll be taking a few notes. Lean slightly forward to show interest in the speaker. Look at the speaker.

I've been told I fidget too much at meetings. Any advice?

Nervous people signal their discomfort by ripping, folding, scribbling on, and crushing everything in sight. To physically prevent you from unconsciously fidgeting at meetings, try the following technique.

Place your writing pad directly in front of you. Imagine an invisible line just beyond it on the table. Place all other objects, such as pens, eyewear, and drinks above the notebook, beyond the invisible line. Whenever you are not actively using these objects, they must remain on the other side of the invisible line. Train yourself to observe this rule and you'll always look cool, calm, and focused.

I cannot stress this enough. Don't play with the edge of your notebook or your papers. I know, I know. Suddenly it becomes exciting to fold the edge of your crisp, white, legal pad back and forth, or even better, to break that empty Styrofoam cup to bits. I hate to be a killjoy, but at the risk of stifling your creative efforts, don't even think of doing any of this. Anymore. Ever.

The meeting has started and the only empty seat is in the front row. How do I walk through the audience?

You don't. This is my opinion, personal and humble as it may be. If the meeting has started and the only open seat is anywhere in the front third of the room, I recommend that you *totally ignore it*. It might as well not be there.

Only during a break, when everyone else gets up, may you take the seat. Until then, stand very still in the back. Let the speaker give the presentation without interruption.

I really have to go to the bathroom. How do I leave a meeting without being too distracting?

At a large meeting, leave quietly, discreetly, and out the nearest door. Your reason for leaving need not be explained; emergencies are generally accepted. When returning, depending on where your seat is, you may need to wait for a break in the presentation. Neither the speaker nor a row of people should be disturbed.

In the smaller environment of a conference room, you may need to ask to be excused as a courtesy: "Please excuse me, I need to step out for a minute," or depending on the formality of the meeting, "Would this be a convenient time?" Of course, you need to choose the moment wisely.

When I get in front of my boss I choke. How can I overcome this?

Fear can be paralyzing. If there's some fear of performing in front of your boss, you can overcome it. What you need is a better relationship. Probably you don't know whether you're doing well or not. You don't know what works. You need to get connected.

Recognizing that part of this disconnect may be from your side. Actively communicate with your boss more than you presently do. Get coworkers' perspectives on the way the office works. Test your ideas with them. Let people know you. Does the boss have an administrative aide or an office manager who acts as a go-between? Get to know that person.

Find someone in your group to be your mentor. Ask for advice and some sense of your performance. How are you viewed? What should you be thinking about? Build up more confidence.

Ask the boss for a review. Your employer should be concerned with developing good people and be ready to help you. Be positive and try the following questions:

- How well am I doing my regular duties?

- How can I improve?

- What could I or should I be doing that I'm not?

- How can I be of greater value to the company?

Be responsive. The key to success in the early stages is to respond to the requests made of you. Listen to the wording and respond on time. Be dependable.

Believe in your ability to handle any criticism and make the changes you need to. If it takes long talks with a friend, or some therapy, do it for yourself. Open up. You have to know what to fix in order to improve. Put these meetings into perspective. Jump out of an airplane over the weekend, then maybe these little meetings won't loom so large.

Meet Your Boss on Your Terms

My boss has called a staff meeting for tomorrow. How can I use the meeting to further my career?

Each appearance you make is an opportunity to show you are ahead of the curve. Find ways to demonstrate your high degree of organization and your ability to think ahead.

Review the last meeting's minutes for your list of responsibilities. Be prepared to report on them in detail. Don't let an item from the previous meeting that has not been completed—or at least addressed—become the focus of this meeting. Handle it prior to the meeting so that it's not made worse by public exposure. Develop your own task and status list, which can be distributed, if appropriate. Systematically review and discuss each item on the list. Add the new things that come up. Keeping visible lists shows you are methodical, organized, and *on it*. See how early you can get the meeting agenda. If there is a new topic, research it so you can discuss it knowledgeably.

My boss called out of the blue with a "Please see me in my office. Now." I am panicking. Do you have any recommendations?

First of all, don't panic. Second, if you disregard that advice and are panicked, no one else needs to know. Do a quick

Ellen's
Hot Tips

Panic Relief Exercise

Whenever you feel like panicking, try this first. Repeat the exercise five times and watch your composure and confidence return.

- Go somewhere private.

- Stand tall.

- Take four deep breaths.

- Swing your arms behind your back and lace your fingers together.

- Keep your arms behind you, fingers laced, as you bend forward at the waist, keeping your back and legs straight.

- Raise your hands toward the ceiling.

- As you bend down, stretching the top of your head toward the floor, exhale gently through your mouth.

- Keep your fingers laced and inhale slowly and deeply through your nose as you slowly begin to stand.

- As your head goes up, your hands go down.

panic relief exercise (see the previous page) to clear your head so you don't feel panicked and anxious. As you stretch and bend over, blood flow increases to your head. The locked-hands position stretches out your spine and expands your chest cavity, allowing more oxygen into your lungs. You will instantly relax and regain more control of your body and mind.

My boss is unhappy about something I've done. How do I stay composed during our meeting?

Although this is an exceptionally good opportunity for crippling paranoia, don't go there. Accept the criticism with cooperation and grace. Defensiveness will only make matters worse. What doesn't kill you will make you stronger. Reassured yet? Prepare to make the best of an unknown situation. With any luck you can learn something useful.

Once in the meeting, your boss may want an honest explanation of the status quo. Lay it out. Don't fudge the facts. If a plan of action is presented, embrace it. There may be new deadlines. Demonstrate that you understand the problem and the solution. Right now, it's "Here's what I can do" or "What can I do?" depending on the situation.

What do you take away from this? Communicate. If you're having trouble with a project or an account, discuss it before the eleventh hour, and seek help. Better to earn respect for anticipation than to lose it for falling short.

I walked into my boss's office. Where do I sit?

Your boss should indicate where you should sit—most likely in the guest chair facing the desk, in one of the chairs at that little round conference table, or on the couch, which always seems strange and bodes no good. In theory, the couch is for a guest of equal or senior status who gets to relax more than you do.

While you wait for instruction, remain standing. If you need room to display your materials, no harm in suggesting the conference seating. "Ira, may we please use the conference table? You'll be better able to view my charts and graphs."

Before you leave, remember to be polite and push your chair in to the table and leave everything as you found it.

I'm in my boss's office and I have my briefcase and my research. Where do I put all of my stuff?

Rooms are settings for certain activities, and the basic office is only for a two- or three-person exchange, without props. You're now forced to work out of your briefcase, from your lap (no good), the floor (terrible), or the other guest chair (so-so), and you'll have to ask permission to use it to be polite.

A larger office may have a small conference table, so you can suggest its use and put your materials there. If you have props, remove your materials from the case and arrange them as you begin. Leave room for your boss's pad. Actually, your boss probably won't bother to get up from his chair. He's preoccupied with the company stock report on his desk. Don't be insulted. Some day you'll be too preoccupied to get up for the junior employee you like. Set your empty case on the floor until you pack to leave.

Think ahead next time. Did you really need the small conference room for this? If so, send your boss a memo and request an appropriate-size room so you can present all your charts and visual aids. Then be sure to reserve the room.

Potpourri

I'm walking into a meeting.
Where should I sit?

Shades of the childhood game of musical chairs. Welcome to the adult world in which where you sit means even more than it did as a child. Scary, isn't it? Follow these simple guidelines scrupulously and you'll be just fine.

Arrive a few minutes early to claim the seat you desire. This doesn't mean you need to sit down, just put your things down to indicate the seat is taken.

The most valuable seats are the ones from which you can see everyone and everything going on. You will also want to be seen, and heard, by both the leadership and the plebes if you choose to contribute.

Do not sit at the head, or end, of the table, unless you are specifically told to sit there. Those seats are reserved for the leaders of the group, as are the seats immediately to their right, respectively. Those seats are for the tried and trusted. Hence, the politically incorrect term "my right-hand man."

Sit in the most powerful position suitable to your status. Where people sit in a meeting can establish their status in the minds of others. Say your office has weekly staff meetings. Carefully observe your particular corporate culture and start by working within those parameters. Once you know the rules, you can break them.

At the first meeting, be sure to observe who sits where. Be cautious about trying a power grab at your very first meeting unless that is precisely the message you want to send.

Do try, however, to sit near the leader(s). You want to be able to listen and observe the big wigs.

Try to watch everything you can. Be a keen observer. It's the best schooling you will ever have.

Remember how much fun it was to sit next to your best friend, or even better, between your two very best friends in school? Remember passing notes and making fun of the teacher? Remember delegating yourselves "Fashion Critics" and joyously ripping everyone apart, in gory detail, especially your teacher? Well, I recommend you *resist the temptation* to sit near anyone you even remotely like or anyone with whom you share a sense of humor. If you are serious about getting down to business, in fact, if you want any career at all, *don't even think of it.*

After the meeting, write down your thoughts and observations. Privately speculate on what you saw. Save these notes in a private, safe space. Read them at some time in the future and see if any of the things you observed and speculated on came to pass. The better you get at this, the more adept your strategies will become.

I am late to a meeting. What should I do?

Consider this. What does it say about you, your values, and your respect for others? Let's see.

- You don't respect anyone in the room.

- You don't respect your colleagues or superiors.

- You don't want a career at this firm beyond this very moment.

- You value your own life, your own time, and the friend you just got off the phone with planning your Caribbean vacation much more than you do this tired old gang.

Hmmm. I'm thinking you might want to apologize immediately and try to catch up.

My cell phone is ringing while someone present is talking. What should I do?

Apologize immediately while reaching for your phone and turning it off. If you are waiting for an urgent call, advise and apologize to the group in advance. Seat yourself at the back of the room, near the exit. If your call does come through, extricate yourself from the room immediately. Try to minimize disturbing everyone else. Once you have completed your cell call, return as unobtrusively as possible.

My boss leaves huge gaps in the conversation. What should I do?

Silence is power. The person who speaks most, longest, and last loses—unless that person is the boss. Use the silence to think about the conversation at hand. Don't waste the time being concerned or self-conscious. Focus and think. You can bet your boss is doing just that—which is how he or she got to be the boss.

I've got to deliver bad news to my boss. How do I break it?

By e-mail from another city may be the easiest way. If that can't be arranged, try the following.

The best way to deliver bad news to your boss is by appointment. In private. Always politely. Discreetly. Briefly. Concisely. The sooner the better. With the appropriate amount of apology, if necessary. With as much forewarning as possible, or none. Gently or forcefully, depending on your boss.

Ask for some time with the boss. State the general subject but no specifics. The less said the better. For example, "There are issues with the Peyton contract we need to discuss." Once you're face to face, get right to the point. Prepare to discuss the real issues. Acknowledge your role, if any. Whether you're part of the problem or not, do your best to understand why this piece of business tanked and what the fixes may be. You may be asked for an opinion, so have one ready.

Finally, thank your boss for taking time with you and leave. Don't slam the door.

Chapter 5

SPEECHES

- Who Are These People?
- What Do They Want from Me?
- You're On Stage Now!
- The Dazzle Is in the Details
- Rehearsal Blues
- Technical Difficulties—
  The Black Hole of Despair
- Potpourri

YOU'VE BEEN POLISHING YOUR SKILLS, HONING your image, and putting the pedal to the metal on the fast track to success. Good for you! But look out, here comes a curve—and it may be a sharp one—sooner or later (probably sooner) someone is going to ask you to give a speech. If you aren't comfortable under the bright lights alone on the stage, it's time to work on your act. To sell

191

your product, you have to sell yourself. And in a roomful of weary listeners, this can require all the skills of a Shakespearian actor and the tenacity of a junkyard dog. Whether this is your first presentation, or just the latest in a long, mind-numbing nightmare of appearances, help is at hand. Turn around, face the footlights, and learn the joy of speaking. Your audience awaits.

Who Are These People?

***How can I possibly know what
the audience cares about?
I have never met them before.***

Speak to them. Get permission to call six to twelve audience members in advance and ask what their challenges are. What keeps them awake at night? What would they like to learn as a result of your presentation? Research their industry, jargon, lingo, and inside issues. Discover who they consider their competition and why. Uncover their needs and their pain. Address these issues and help them solve their problems. They will love you forever and keep inviting you back. Ask your event planner to contact those he or she has provided to you so they will be expecting your call. Then make those calls. Here are some questions you may want to ask:

- What do you feel is the biggest concern of the audience members who will be at this program as it relates to your topic? Why?

- How have these issues been addressed in the past?

- Can you think of an example of someone who has dealt successfully with this issue already?

- How did he or she do it?

- What recent changes might have caused the audience members' concerns?

After each question you'll want to probe some more and get details. When writing your speech, consider using some of the actual examples from these telephone interviews. This will make a big impact. For example, to reinforce a point, you might say, "As a matter a fact, Dr. Daniel Rubenstein in your Princeton University office shared that _____." This is particularly important when you are an outside speaker.

You may want to include the boss, president, CEO, or a few people at the top level of the group when conducting your telephone interview. It always helps to get the take of these people, plus you now have direct access to a key person in the organization.

How can I target my speech to my audience?

Thoroughly investigate and research your audience prior to giving your speech. You need to know their demographics, values, and, most important, their pain. After creating your vision for your speech, the next step is to research your topic. This gives you the support material you need to "sell" your idea or concept to the audience. In some cases that research may already be done for you. In other situations you may need to "flush out" your topic so that you give the audience some kind of substantive proof that your view is the one they should take. You will need to do topic-specific research and audience-specific research.

> **Topic-specific research.** You can find information to support your presentation in a variety of places including the Internet, trade journals and periodicals, books, quotes, surveys and reports, government or association statistics, and so on. If your company or organization has conducted any kind of research, you'll want to consider incorporating some of that information in your speech if it helps you make your point.

> **Audience-specific research.** In addition to researching your topic, it is critical to fully understand the needs of your audience. This helps you gear your presentation in both substance and style to the very group you wish to influence. Ask the person in charge

of the event where you'll be giving your speech for demographic information about that audience. You'll want to know percentage of men and women, age ranges, education level, income levels, and so on.

What Do They Want from Me?

How can I motivate my audience?

After you conduct research on your audience, you'll know who they are and how to motivate them. In short, find their pain and help them resolve it. Reward them with what they want: exposure, acknowledgment, a way to increase their income, education, whatever. Speak to their values and their hearts.

How can I get my audience in the mood to hear my speech?

First and foremost, have a good presenter give you a good introduction. Research your audience so you know what will get them in the mood. Use that up front. Warm them up with your most recent embarrassing situation. I don't often recommend extensive stories and slides of your last family vacation.

I want the audience to like me. What can I do?

Competently use the time and trust that your audience gives you, and they will like you. They will really like you if you remember to do these things:

- Engage the audience.

- Help them solve some of the challenges they are facing.

- Speak to their hearts. Speak to their sense of humor.

- Help them feel good about themselves.

- Before the meeting starts, meet and greet. Mingle. Create some friends.

- Use language they use.

- Use "we" instead of "I."

- Empathize with them.

- Mention what you learned in your research.

- Have lots of audience participation. Use volunteers. Give volunteers small gifts.

Try to shorten the distance between yourself and your audience. Speak to each person. Let your eyes settle on their eyes and hold their attention. By creating intimacy with one person, the rest of the audience feels intimacy with you, too.

What if the audience asks me questions?

What if they don't? Ideally, your audience will be full of questions, which you will regard as great praise. A show of interest is proof they listened to what you said, are interested, and value your expertise.

If there is even a remote possibility you will take questions from the audience, rehearse the answers you want to give to the questions you think they will ask, including potentially embarrassing or difficult questions. Prepare and rehearse your answers.

Sometimes the greatest challenge with Q&A is getting someone in the audience to ask that very first question. Don't panic if it takes a moment. In fact, expect it to take

Leadership from the Audience

Ellen's Hot Tips

Remember this moment of transition from speaker speaking to audience asking questions the next time you are in an audience. Show your leadership abilities and be the generous audience member who helps the speaker break the ice with the first question from the audience. Every speaker will be grateful to you and always request your presence in the audience.

a moment for the audience to realize that it is now their turn to speak and to find their voice. A great way to get things moving is to plant a few questions in the audience. Once the ice is broken, it becomes easier for others.

The audience is embarrassed for you if no one asks questions. So have the first question and answer ready. For example, you can get them started by saying, "Well, the question I get most often is _____." Then you can say, "Does anyone know the answer?" Be gentle, or select someone, pull him up by the scruff of his neck, and put him on the spot. "You, sir, in the blue suit, you're on."

Should I interact with the audience or is that too risky?

The risk comes in *not* interacting. Go for it, baby. Make their day. And yours. Remember, as speaker and presenter, you are in control. Own it. Interact.

You're On Stage Now!

How can I come across as a good communicator?

How you communicate sends a message about your professionalism, your credibility, and your education. Or lack thereof.

It is increasingly common for Americans to use unprofessional, unrefined, unsophisticated language, trendy words, and even profanity. This grammar and vocabulary may be acceptable on the street, but it is not recommended within the business culture.

I am a techie nerd and proud of it, but my manager says I'm boring people to death. What do you recommend?

Try this easy layering technique to get started painlessly. Add emotion and take a talk from boring to interesting and involving. Here is how you do it.

Begin with the fact.	I have an idea.
Personalize it.	*Mr. Schneider,* I have an idea.
Add emotional adjectives.	Mr. Schneider, I have a *great* idea.
Explain the value.	Mr. Schneider, I have a great idea *for increasing our sales.*

My quarterly review said I sound like I am reciting a speech, not sharing real information. How can I sound more real?

The good news is that you do seem to know your information thoroughly. That's a great first step.

The way to get away from sounding like you are "reciting a speech" is to make the information real to yourself. This means adding emotional value to the different bits of information. Attach value and importance to what is important, as you do naturally in real life. Glide through what is not as important. Emphasize and repeat what you need your audience to remember. Stress specific words to emphasize your points. Make the most of your vocal capacity.

In acting it is always better to give too much and have the director rein you in. Be bold. Go for the gusto. Be big. It will feel really awkward, even ridiculous, at first. But I promise, it works.

I want to look good when I give my speech. What should I wear?

Wear clothes in which you can move comfortably and in which you feel terrific. Wear colors that look great on you. Choose flattering colors that don't overshadow you. Be careful not to go overboard and wear something too bright, too wild, or too patterned, which will only distract the audience from your face and your message.

Be mindful to frame your face with both colors and patterns appropriate to the specific situation and circumstance. The tie for a man and a scarf or a necklace for a woman are powerful tools. They should be used to attract and focus attention to your face.

How can I give myself a pep talk to psych myself up?

When I work with clients, we create and fill their personal "tool chest" with emotional triggers and pep talk affirmations (or sayings, for you non–New Age stuffed shirts) to get them through the day, the talk, the difficult situations.

Ellen's
Hot Tips

Stocking Your Pep Talk Tool Chest

Here are some pep talk tool chest sense memory trigger suggestions. Use these and create your own to stimulate a great feeling in your soul. Then revisit or relish the feelings that this memory evokes.

- Remember the time you drove in the winning run.

- Remember how you felt when you met the love of your life.

- Remember the time you aced a test you didn't study for.

- Remember how it felt to close your first major deal.

- Remember how it felt to receive a compliment for work well done from an otherwise distant boss.

Do this for yourself now. See "Stocking Your Pep Talk Tool Chest" for ways to fill your own tool chest of affirmations.

A pep talk or self-talk is fun. Get into it. Talk to yourself in an encouraging way to get your emotions moving in a positive way. Speak to your heart. Create emotional sentences or fragments that move your heart and soul. Use your emotional and sense memory, smells and tastes, photos and fabrics, whatever gets you going.

Sometimes the memory of a specific event or a moment in time may trigger a memory strong enough to pep you up. Actors call this "sense memory."

It helps if you write your ideas in a notebook or journal so you can continue to grow with them, work with them, and hone the list so each and everything on it really inspires you. The more you use and revisit these items, the more useless or workable they will become for you. Keep and use only those pep triggers that work consistently. Treat them with supreme care; they are your precious gifts. Treat them like the family jewels. (Note: Just so you know, actors think it's bad luck to share their personal sense memory triggers. Except with me, of course!)

I'm about to give a speech. I feel like I am going to throw up! What can I do?

Throw up. It's the best thing you can do. Better out than in, as my father always says. And certainly it's best to do it sooner, preferably in the bathroom, than later on stage. (And it's yet another good reason to carry your toothbrush, toothpaste, mints, and mouthwash. Use them all in this particular case, and I don't mean sparingly.) Vomit and move on. You don't have to tell anyone. Then refocus on the business at hand.

By the way, congratulations are in order. You have now joined the ranks of some of the best and brightest politicians, celebrities, and leaders of all time. Some actors throw up every night. Now you know you are merely human and nervous. No worries.

I finished my speech! How do I exit gracefully?

Smile, look out at your very pleased audience, and give them a warm "Thank you," nod slightly to show deference, and then gracefully walk off stage (to whichever side you have previously arranged).

The Dazzle Is in the Details

I'm trying to write a speech. Where do I start?

There are two different perspectives I like to use when writing a speech.

Begin with your goals in mind. If your goal is to share your body of knowledge with an audience who knows very little about the field in which you are an expert, write the speech from your vantage point.

Research your audience and speak to their needs. If you are to report to an involved sales force about their numbers this season and educate them about the newest product line for fall, write from their vantage point.

Either way, you must make your information relevant to your audience.

How can I research the needs of my audience and focus on them in my speech?

One way to uncover the needs and concerns of your audience is with a written survey. This should be brief, perhaps five to ten questions. In some cases you'll want multiple-choice answers or simple fill in the blanks. Not only will you get an indication as to what concerns and issues you're audience members have, but you can also use that survey to support the points you make in your speech. "According to the survey I took prior to addressing you, 75 percent of you felt that _____." This gives your speech a feeling of authenticity.

Ellen's Believe It or Not

I once had a client who was asked to give a sales and marketing speech by an association of boat manufacturers. The audience was independent boat dealers. After conducting a telephone survey with some of the potential audience members, my client discovered the big issue for this audience: They felt the prospects for new boat sales were going to be slow for the upcoming season. And, since they were all small businesses, they couldn't afford to advertise any more than they already were.

My client started going through the association surveys and trade journals and discovered an interesting piece of information. The survey showed that 12 percent of current boat owners said they would be in the market for a new boat within the next twelve months. If you had 1,000 customers in your database, my client concluded that it was reasonable to assume that 120 of them might be in the market to buy a boat over the next year. These statistics were critical in getting the audience to accept the premise of the speech, which was to focus first on your own customer base for new sales before spending a fortune generating new customers.

What are the most important elements to consider when writing a speech or presentation?

There are actually eighteen steps to a good speech. Check them off before you give your next presentation.

1. **Organize your material.** One of the most common places people make mistakes is in the organization of their presentation. They aren't clear on which information the audience will want to hear first.

2. **State your goal to the audience.** Tell your audience what you are going to tell them. Tell them. Tell them what you just told them. You have heard this before because it works. Try it.

3. **Prioritize your information.** You must prioritize so people hear the most critical material right up front. Audiences form their impressions and decisions within the *first 5 to 15 seconds* of your presentation, so you need to hit them with your good stuff first.

4. **Get to the point.** Don't get bogged down in details. I often see up-and-coming leaders make this mistake. They are so proud of all the work they have done that they go on and on with all the details of

how they got there. Your audience doesn't have the time or interest. They want you to get to the point.

5. **Write down the technical information and hand it out.** If you have a great deal of technical information you want your audience to know, provide them with handouts or manuals. Audience members who want additional information can learn more on their own or speak to you privately. Present technical material in an interesting way. Technical information is complex, specific, and, when presented poorly, excruciatingly dull.

6. **Use descriptive adjectives.** Bland, dry information turns audiences off immediately. Instead of "Our model 2273C has a 5.2GHz processor, four expansion slots, and a 16-inch multiscan flat-panel LCD," say, "We are proud to share with you our newest processor, which is one of the most powerful and fastest in the entire industry. Now we're excited to show you how fast that really is."

7. **Skip the jargon.** If you speak in jargon, unless it is to your peers, chances are you will lose your audience—quickly. No matter how much you think you have taken out the jargon, you need to have a person outside your field review your writing. And no, this doesn't mean your spouse or best friend, who have been around you enough to pick up

your jargon. Have an outsider, or a coach, review all of your presentations to make sure every point is communicated clearly and can be easily understood.

8. **When in doubt, leave it out.** Many of us are so immersed in our fields we forget that most people won't grasp the information that comes so naturally to us, let alone enjoy hearing it.

9. **Personalize information.** Give credit freely. Make your information relevant to your audience by personalizing it. Instead of saying, "Branch customers made 3,200 transactions with us since we last met," say, "Mary and John, you are responsible for more than doubling the number of transactions customers made at your branch since our last meeting. Congratulations, this means so much to our bank. At national headquarters, we recognize the significance of the substantial increase in these numbers."

10. **Express emotion.** It doesn't mean you are a weenie or weak. If you are able to interject energy, passion, and emotion, your audience will be much more likely to listen and buy into what you are saying. Granted, it may be difficult for some people to speak with emotion any of the time. And it may be difficult for all people to speak

with emotion all of the time. But it is best if all people speak with emotion most of the time. Even those we normally consider tough and free of emotion—some of the most motivating, inspirational, emotional speeches have been made by powerful military men before battle.

11. **Sell to emotions.** People make decisions intellectually, but they buy emotionally. When you are speaking, you are selling something—yourself, your ideas, your products.

12. **Tell a story.** Turning your information into a story helps your audience bond with you. Tell a story close to your heart and you'll find your audience warming to you. Always make sure the story is relevant to the situation.

13. **Don't misuse humor.** If you aren't comfortable using humor, ad-libbing, or using personal anecdotes, don't. Consider incorporating quotes from famous people or tell anecdotes honoring your colleagues, bosses, or predecessors.

14. **Choose your words carefully.** Select your words carefully. Set an example for others.

15. **Humanize the numbers.** Explain their meaning and relevance to your audience. Create examples that illustrate your numbers and their meanings.

Share information so the audience will relate to the cold, hard facts. Don't say: "The Web site had more than 1,200,000 hits last month." Instead, say: "Our Web site had more than a million hits last month, which means we reached more customers last month than all of the previous six months combined. This translated into sales figures that exceeded our expectations, allowing us to expand three departments. It also allowed some of you to hire those assistants you truly deserve."

16. **Compare and contrast.** Comparing and contrasting provides a framework for your information and can help the audience understand and follow what you are saying. You might compare yourself to a competitor by saying, "Our sales increased by 80.5 percent from last year while ArchRival Consultants increased by only 48 percent."

17. **Provide direction and motivation with specifics.** Providing direction gives your audience a frame of reference by showing where you are now and where you can go. Instead of saying, "We'll be able to manage 800 clients," you might say, "We're currently managing 200 clients in our division. After the buyout, we can quadruple this figure almost immediately."

18. Call to action. Toward the end of your presentation, you will want to ask your audience to take a specific action. A call to action can be as simple as asking for a vote, a donation, or approval. To be more effective, give them not only your call to action but also the specific steps of the process. For example: "So, when you walk into that voting booth and close the curtain next Tuesday, look over the list of candidates and pull the lever for Smith."

What is a good way to address the audience for the first time at the beginning of my speech?

Put your best verbal foot forward. What is in a greeting? Everything. Just as I have described in this book the importance of making a good first impression and all the important variables involved, your initial greeting to your audience has a powerful and lasting effect on their receptivity to you, their mood, and their response to you going forward. In creating a strong, bonding greeting for your audience, consider including some of these facts:

- The time of your address
- The agenda of the meeting and what is before and after your presentation
- The mood of the audience in the moment

- The weather outside
- The purpose of this meeting
- The message you have prepared
- Any current local or regional news
- Any big national or international news
- Something your boss, the client, or meeting planner wants you to say
- The number of people in your audience
- The status of the audience as well as their demographics

Ellen's Essentials

One of the most gracious welcomes I have heard recently was voiced by Deepak Chopra at the beginning of a huge weekend seminar: "Thank you for being here. It is a great honor and privilege to be here with you and spend the next few days together."

What did I like? Despite Chopra's celebrity status and worldwide renown, he chose to be very humble, express his appreciation to us as his audience, and generously give us high status as his audience—whether we deserved it or not.

What if I lose my place while speaking?

Simply accept the fact you lost your place and refocus as quickly as possible. Calmly find your place, smile at your audience as if you are doing exactly what you had planned, and continue on. No one else need know the poignant pause was unplanned.

Later, to prevent this from happening again, evaluate what happened and find a way to correct it. Recognize why you lost your place. Were you focused on your material? Were you stating it with passion and purpose? Were you watching and listening to your audience? Did you know what you were saying and why? Had you done your research? Had you written out your speech, then outlined or bulleted it for this presentation? Had you taken care of the physical requirements your body needed to do its best? Answering these questions, and working on the mistakes they uncover, will help you be better prepared the next time.

Rehearsal Blues

I want my speech to sound natural. Should I just skip rehearsing it?

No! No! NO! The most natural-sounding speeches sound natural because they are extremely well rehearsed. Think about it. Actors have weeks of rehearsal before they are practiced enough to sound natural and unrehearsed.

Rehearsal is a critical part of preparing for your speech. Ironically, it is a step most business people cut short or ignore completely. Can you imagine Marlon Brando, Tom Hanks, or Julia Roberts doing a movie without rehearsing? Unthinkable.

Am I the only person who hates rehearsing for these presentations I have to give?

No. Most business people complain vehemently about rehearsing and have no time for it. Compare them to actors, who tend to love rehearsal. As you learn the fun, freedom, and power of a professional rehearsal, it's my hope that you will totally change your mind.

What's enjoyable about a rehearsal?

Everything—if you are doing it right. A good rehearsal can provide the most creative, liberating, and playful time of your life. Yes. Really.

Rehearsal gives you a whole new latitude for being. A great rehearsal provides an opportunity to:

- Use both sides of your brain

- Explore your hidden and vulnerable heart

- Exercise your imagination

- Focus your full mental capacity

- Direct your physical energy

- Determine what action you want your audience to take

Before your first rehearsal, prime the pump. Describe your vision. Define your goals. Once you are ready to work,

Rehearse with Emotion

Ellen's Hot Tips

One great technique I adapted from my theater and TV experience really helps clients in rehearsal. This exercise for emotional variation helps you build layers to your performance, and it is these emotional layers that add power and energy to your speeches. I am not suggesting that you ever make a speech in any one, specific emotion, but this exercise takes you through a variety of them and will help make your presentations more dynamic.

(continues)

(continued)

Read the script in several different emotions. Rehearse your script seductively. Then read it with anger. Try a few more emotions—fear, shame, aggression, and timidity. The more dramatic, or stronger, the emotional commitment, the better.

It sounds weird, I know. But it works. Try it wholeheartedly. Commit to it and see what comes up for you. You will be surprised at how, from moment to moment, different emotions evoke different readings, and the different readings provoke different audience response.

By rehearsing this way, you benefit from sense memory. You have experienced all the varied emotions you can access, and you can bring these emotional elements into your speech when you need to. Remember, this exercise is not designed to provoke emotional response in you. You want to evoke emotional response from your audience.

think about whom you will be addressing. Identifying your audience will help you select the most appropriate information, language, and even anecdotes and humor to use. If the audience is not familiar with your field, you will need to speak in language they understand and with which they identify. If the audience consists of your peers or people with your technical expertise, you will be able to include more technical information. However, keep in mind that just because an audience understands your technical talk doesn't mean they will be interested in extremely detailed presentations. Bland, dry information turns off an audience immediately. Use descriptive adjectives, body language, and vocal variety to convey energy.

I'm giving my first big speech. What's the best way to rehearse?

The trick—as with so many things—is to videotape yourself and observe your own speech as an outsider. Pretend the person in your video is someone else. View the tape and ask yourself these questions:

- Do I believe what this person is saying?

- Do I trust and respect this person?

- Do I want to hear more?

- Is this person likeable?

- Is the presentation clear? Understandable?

- Is this person enthusiastic about the topic?

Watch the video a few times straight through, knowing that you, like everyone else, will probably hate seeing yourself on video. Remember, this is how everyone else sees you, so it is important both personally and professionally that you be aware of how you really appear.

On the positive side, I will now guide you through a method for reviewing these tapes so you begin to love watching yourself and feel positive about your looks, verbal acuity, composure, and body language. This is a great opportunity to embrace your good habits and praise yourself. It's also your chance to clean up anything that does not present your best. Have a pen and paper handy to make notes as you go. It is helpful to track your progress and target your opportunities for growth. Here's how to get the most from your review:

- First, turn the sound off completely and watch your body language. Look for powerful, positive, believable gestures and postures. Less movement is better until you are trained in professional presentation. Also check for annoying habits you might not be aware of.

- Second, replay the tape as you close your eyes and listen. Hear how you sound without the benefit of the visual component. Listen for your best examples of vocal inflection, variety, melody, speed, pacing, pauses, and punch. Here's the time to notice and correct those bad little verbal habits, such as overuse of "umms," "errrrs," and "aahs." Listen for awkward phrasing, mispronounced words, mumbling, folksy expressions, slang, jargon, and colloquialisms.

- You have gotten this far and you're good. Let's make you even better. Rewind your video once again and listen as you view it. Make notes on what you would like to do to improve your performance and incorporate those ideas into the next run-through.

- Rehearse completely; don't leave things out.

Break your script down into bite-size segments. Practice the beginning until you're comfortable. Then practice the

---

Ellen's Believe It or Not

Why is it important to videotape yourself?

I once had a very senior level corporate executive client who had the annoying habit of grabbing his unmentionables while speaking—let's call it the "Michael Jackson syndrome." His staff was afraid to tell him. As his speaking coach, it was my responsibility to discreetly eliminate this problem. I videotaped him, and then left him alone to review the tape. When I returned, I could see he was painfully aware of what he had been doing. I never had to mention it to him, and it never was a problem from that point forward.

---

ending, or "the close," to ensure that you'll end with a bang. Next, depending on how long your speech is, break up the middle in small sections and practice each of them individually. Once you feel comfortable with the different segments, you can start putting them together, in the proper order, of course.

When rehearsing, make the words and the audience real for you. There is no difference for a professional actor—nor should there be for you—between rehearsing and performing.

I don't want to look like I'm reading. Should I use a script?

Whether you use a script or not, you never want look or sound as though you are reading. Prior to the event, with the audience position firmly established in your mind, practice reading your speech one sentence at a time. Start saying the first part of the sentence as you raise your head and your eyes to the audience. Finish the sentence with your eyes on someone in your imaginary audience. Start the next sentence with your head up and eyes out. Then, as you need to, glance down and grab the next chunk of script. Lift your eyes to your adoring audience and share your profound bits of information. If you train yourself to look up as soon and as much as possible, it will become a habit. The way you rehearse becomes the way you present.

The trickiest parts are at the beginning and end of the speech. The beginning is tough because you're nervous with expectation. Once you're into it, the middle is usually great. Toward the end of the speech, people often get tired and forget this "head-up, eyes-out method" and fall into the incredibly boring "nonmethod method" of literally reading their script. You can do better.

If you're the spontaneous type, try bullet points. You may do your best rehearsing with a fully scripted document and then bullet point only when you are presenting. On the other hand, you may prefer to have the script in its entirety in front of you when speaking, for security, even if you never look at it. If you do want to use bullet points for the ultimate delivery, practice with them many times to make sure you have the full content at your disposal.

How do I prepare my notes for on-stage use?

When printing your script for use on stage, employ these tips and make it easy for yourself:

- Use only the top half of the page. This way you won't be looking so far down the page and the audience won't be looking at your bald spot. It will also be easier for you to look up at your audience and create eye contact.

- Use large (14-point) type in a serif font (that's one like Times New Roman, where each letter leads you into the next one).

- Use wide margins to make it easy to read.

Ellen's Hot Tips

The Handwriting on the Script

If you are working on a specific behavioral modification issue, I encourage you to make notes to yourself in the margins of the final copy of your speech. For example, if you are working on speaking more slowly, you may want to write "slowly" on either the left or right margin of the page. Similarly, if you forget to smile or pause when you need to, write "smile" or "pause" where you need to do that. Use one side of your script consistently so you don't have to bother searching for your cues or prompts during your delivery.

I strongly recommend writing these notes by hand in the margins. Why, you might ask? Although I have never had one of my clients do this, I have seen these "stage directions" accidentally end up being read aloud by a nervous speaker as part of the speech content. If typed and bracketed in the text of the speech, there is a greater chance of error. This is very embarrassing for both speaker and audience.

- Double space. This will help you see the copy but also gives you space to write in additions if you get some new information that you want to include in your speech after you have already printed it out.

- Always number your pages in the unhappy event your script gets scattered.

- Bring an extra copy of your speech. Keep it in a separate location. Have one copy in your briefcase and carry an extra copy in your suitcase.

- If you're traveling, make sure one copy of your script, any audio visual aids you'll be using, and any important handouts are in your carry-on luggage. If you expect to make last minute changes, have your speech on a notebook computer and bring your own travel printer and paper.

Technical Difficulties— The Black Hole of Despair

How do I prepare visual aids to look great, enhance my talk, and keep things interesting?

Visual aids can be a great addition to your program. Use these suggestions to be sure they support your talk and work for your audience.

- Be sure to limit the number of graphics you use. Rule of thumb: no more than three per minute.

- Make them colorful and easy to read.

- Bullets are more effective than full sentences.

- Each slide should contain no more than three bullet points.

- Don't make the type too small. Rule of thumb: font size 14 or larger. Remember, people in the back of the room will need to read your visuals.

- Always make time for a run-through before the actual presentation.

- Don't stand between the projector and the screen, or your slides will be projected onto your body.

- Don't turn out the lights. You're making it too easy for your audience to fall asleep.

I'm nervous about being the center of attention. Can I use slides and PowerPoint so people aren't looking at me?

Use all the props you want, but people will still be looking at you. Even using extensive visual aids, you will indeed be the center of attention. You are the human element and therefore the most interesting and constantly changing part of the presentation. Having said this, let's address your real issue here.

To help you master your nervousness, take some quiet time and ask yourself why you feel this way. Do you associate being the center of attention with past negative experiences? This is the very source of the problem for many people. Were you embarrassed or shamed as a child during an attempt at speaking? Discovering the cause of this issue will help you resolve it.

Next, diffuse your emotional triggers. This takes time, commitment, and compassion for yourself. It may take

Ellen's Believe It or Not

Although very tall and very handsome, a successful architect with a minor speech impediment was painfully shy. As a child, his parents told him to hold himself back so as not to overshadow his younger brother. As a result, he held himself back not just in childhood but in his adult life as well. Recently, when asked to be the president of a small board of directors, he took a big leap of faith and said "yes" rather than his customary "no."

For him, it was the right time to face his fear and shyness, advance his career, and broaden his life. Now he speaks routinely to groups and chairs several large organizations, and he loves every minute he is the center of attention.

help from friends, parents or relatives, or professionals. Your efforts are well worth it if you can free yourself from these nagging doubts and insecurities. I know there is a confident stage presence waiting to emerge. Let that sassy little boy/girl out.

To overcome stifling natural shyness, choose to take a bold step. Try something new and challenging. Make the decision and go for it!

I am delivering a speech and someone's cell phone is ringing. Should I react?

You have no choice but to react. Everyone is hearing it. Everyone is disturbed and distracted. However, you are the speaker. You have the control. So you handle it. Don't stress out. While no one needs this sort of distracting element, it is easily handled.

This is a great lesson. Next time, remember to ask the audience before you start to turn off their cell phones.

Consider it an opportunity to win over your audience by having some fun at the expense of the poor sap who inadvertently left his or her phone on. Your objective is to quickly deal with this unfortunate interruption and gracefully redirect your audience to the subject at hand using humor.

Use the following "practiced" ad libs or, better yet, create your own humorous responses. For example, "Okay. Let's put those cell phones and pagers on vibrator mode

Ellen's Believe It or Not

If an audience member's cell phone rings right in the middle of the speech and the owner is near the front of the room, I have a client who will actually go to that person and ask for the phone. My client then answers the cell phone, has a brief conversation along the lines of "Hello. He's a little busy right now. Sure. Okay, I'll tell him." He then hangs up the cell phone, hands it back to the audience member, and says with a straight face—loud enough for everyone to hear—"It was the doctor's office. They said don't worry about the rash." His audiences roar with laughter.

You can dispel the tension of a cell phone ringing with a little bit of humor while winning over your audience.

and your vibrators on pager mode." Or, "Next person whose cell phone goes off will be my next volunteer."

Audiences respond very well to humor, and this keeps you, the speaker, in control.

What if the audiovisual people don't show up?

Curse them heavily under your breath and swear never to use them again. Then, fall back on your carefully prepared plan for this "unexpected" situation.

Unfortunately, this is a common problem. I hate this reality but it's true. So you'd better have an alternative and complete presentation ready that doesn't need audiovisuals just in case it happens to you.

If your presentation relies heavily on your audiovisuals, as mine always does, it's a very difficult transition you must make quickly and flawlessly. If you can add humor, do. The more, the better. It will break the tension and aid in the transition.

There are several options, depending on your situation, professional demands, and personal style. If you have handouts, you may rely more heavily on them. If you had planned to use many charts and graphs, you will have to skip some of the facts, figures, and, of course, all the references to the slides or overheads. If appropriate, furnish the information for your audience as soon as possible.

Potpourri

Should I take questions as they come or have a Q&A after my presentation?

There is no right answer; only personal preference. But most speakers prefer a Q&A at the end of a speech, which allows the speaker to get through all of the material as planned. This format provides you with maximum control over the way the material is presented. This format also prevents the audience from derailing your train of thought and asking questions you would have answered in your speech.

Announce the format, whatever it is, at the very beginning of the meeting or speech so your audience will know how to conduct themselves.

How can I memorize my speech? Or should I try?

You certainly want to know your material inside out. You must know how and why you scripted your talk the way you

Ellen's Special Speaking Water for a Perfect Presentation

Ellen's Hot Tips

Ingredients:

Evian Water (or any nonbubbly water) at room temperature. No ice.

1 fresh squeezed lemon. Squeeze carefully—be sure you have no seeds.

1 flexible straw, already flexed.

did. But I don't usually recommend that you memorize your speech unless you are a professional speaker or entertainer. Don't even think of it. It's not worth the time or energy.

The key to being a great speaker or being a normal person able to give a great presentation is that you must make the words and the message sound as if it is coming out of you spontaneously at that very moment. To do that, you must be fully present (mind, body, and spirit), and committed to sharing this great message with your audience. Ironic as it may seem, whether you memorize each word or get the main points down and wing it from there, your best speaking will *appear* to be done spontaneously.

I just found out where I'm giving the speech. Should I go check it out?

Absolutely. In fact, always check out the venue as soon as possible. Where you speak makes a big difference in how you speak. For example, think of how differently you might speak and behave in each of these situations: when speaking to a close colleague in the privacy, comfort, and safety of your own office; speaking to a group of 25 college students on a tour; or speaking to a live international audience from the White House Rose Garden.

Get the idea? The "where" does make a substantial difference in the "how" and sometimes the "what." Check out the venue ASAP.

Checklist for the Venue

You may give a perfect presentation, but if something goes wrong at the venue with the sound system or the lighting, your speech might not even be heard! To guarantee your message makes the maximum impact, find out as much about the meeting site and the audiovisual system as possible.

1. Go early. See what is already set up.

2. Make friends with the crew and the techies.

3. Try out the microphone.

4. Stand on stage. Walk around using all the space you are given.

5. Get the feel of the room. Check out the "vibes."

6. Find your key light (the main light that illuminates your face).

7. Determine where to stand so you are in it.

8. Make sure there is a place for you, or an assistant, to put a glass and a pitcher full of Ellen's Special Speaking Water on the shelf in the lectern prior to your speaking.

What do I do when I have the stage and disaster strikes?

You need to have a plan. Nothing can be more disruptive to your speech than to have something go wrong, especially a disaster. As soon as there is some kind of disturbance, be aware that the audience will be totally focused on it and not on you. However, as the cool, calm leader that you are, you can turn this negative into a tremendous positive. Remember: She who is on stage, rules the world.

Your first strategy for dealing with potential disasters is to do whatever you can to prevent them. No matter how much you anticipate problems and do what you can to prevent them, it is inevitable that things will go wrong. This is when your preparation is even more important.

Create a few humorous lines and keep them tucked away for such events. From your audience's perspective, it will look like you came up with these lines off the top of your head. In reality, you have prepared them in advance and perhaps used them before. Since the line appears to be ad-libbed, it doesn't have to be hilarious to get a good response. Mildly amusing will do. Not only will you get a laugh, but these lines will also help you regain the focus of your audience and win them over just a little bit more. To give you some idea of what a "rehearsed ad-lib" is, here are a few examples that have been used by my clients. Use these or create your own.

Microphone doesn't work. Use mock sign language.

Sound is bad in the back. Usually someone in the back will yell out that they can't hear. You say in a mock yelling tone, "I said, people who are hard of hearing are oversexed!"

Ellen's Believe It or Not

Speaking to a group of retailers, a professional marketing expert was forewarned by management not to bring up a new corporate policy that was causing a major rift with their retail customers. Sure enough, the first question he got was about this new policy. Brilliant at ad-libbing, he responded adroitly, "That's obviously a very important issue to everyone in this room. But before I answer that, I would first like to deal with an issue slightly less controversial. I'd like to share my views on abortion."

My client, the speaker, told me later that as those words came out of his mouth he realized he might have made a huge mistake.

Luckily, everyone laughed. The humor diffused a potentially volatile situation. Management hired him again because he had handled himself and the audience so gracefully without missing a beat.

Microphone has interference. "This is a broadcast from outer space. We are waiting for signs of intelligent life."

Lights go out. "I hope everyone brought a date."

Waiter drops tray of glasses. "Mazel Tov!" (Works well in Florida, Los Angeles, and New York.)

The boss can't make it. He wants me to fill in for him and give his speech. How do I stand in?

Congratulations! Recognize this as a big vote of confidence from your boss. It's a great opportunity for you to use all the things you have been learning and do your boss proud. Breathe deeply and don't panic. You can do this.

Call in a professional coach. A professional coach will know how to maximize your time, orchestrate rehearsals, and make sure you do the best, most professional job possible in the limited time available. This is well worth the expense, even if you pay for it yourself. Make use of this great opportunity and do yourself, your boss, and your organization proud.

If on your own, here's what to do. If your boss wants you to read his or her speech, get a copy of it immediately and start to practice. The more time you have to rehearse, the better. Get permission to use an office (or a private room) and close the door. Hold all calls, unless it's the boss.

First, read the speech aloud, as you would normally read something you have never read before. This way you get an experience of it, purely as the reader. Next, read the speech over and over for the information it contains. Analyze it. Discover what, in your opinion, your boss wanted the audience to learn. Break down the speech into sections to help yourself define the areas of interest and importance.

A technique called "as if" is often used by actors to get into character, and it may be very useful here. Review the speech "as if" you were your boss. Get into his or her head, needs, goals, and objectives. Emphasize whatever you think your boss would have. Practice giving the speech.

Try to create some humorous first line that ties into your boss's absence and how you are filling in in your boss's place.

If you have to write the speech, ask your boss who you should go to for help and guidance regarding company information, the tone of the speech, information on what has been done in the past, what was successful, what failed, and why.

Don't worry yourself too much. You can do this. Welcome this opportunity as a gift. Then get out there and practice all you have learned. Good luck!

Why would I bother with a professional coach when I can get friends' advice and read up on this?

Your brother, mother, sister, aunt, cousin, ex-sister-in-law once removed by marriage and then divorced and then remarried all know they can do as good a job, if not better, than a professional coach. Right? Here is why you are the smart one if you smile politely, listen courteously to their advice, then promptly call me or another professional coach.

No professional athlete would ever conceive of planning and working to be the best without years of professional coaching. If you are getting down to business and want to fast track your career, make a commitment to learning from the best.

Expedite your way to the top by actively seeking out professional guidance whether in the form of reading, group classes, individual coaching, or finding a mentor or coach. Make yourself proud. Plan and actively seek out professional advice, guidance, and coaching. As my friend and mentor Zig Ziglar always says, "See you at the top!"

INDEX

About the Author

ELLEN A. KAYE is one of the nation's leading experts on effective presentation skills, leadership image development, and communication and media skills. Her knowledge and expertise make her one of the most sought-after coaches and speakers today.

Before forming Perfect Presentation, her professional career- and life-coaching service, Ellen acted, modeled, and did voice-overs, as well as directed, produced, and edited in both New York and Los Angeles. She has acted in several soap operas and movies and has appeared in more than 350 national television commercials for clients including American Express, AT&T, Carnival Cruise, Citibank, Colgate Palmolive, and others. She has also posed for numerous magazine covers, posters, billboards, and print ads for top clients across the country.

Ellen holds a B.A. in history from Stanford University. Her company, Perfect Presentation, is located in Scottsdale, Arizona. She is a member of National Speaker's Association, Screen Actors Guild, Actor's Equity Association, American Federation of Television and Radio Artists, and the Author's Guild.

Ellen is a vivacious, informative, and inspiring speaker and coach. Her extensive media and theater experience make her a natural. She is available for keynote addresses, workshops, break-out sessions, group training, seminars, executive retreats, and individual coaching.

Ellen A. Kaye
Perfect Presentation
P.O. Box 6064
Scottsdale, Arizona 85258-6064
Phone: 480-391-9888
Fax: 480-661-9777
E-mail: Ellen@ellenkaye.com
Website: www.ellenkaye.com